Better Homes and Gardens®

OUTSIDE
YOUR HOUSE

BETTER HOMES AND GARDENS® BOOKS

Editor: Gerald M. Knox
Art Director: Ernest Shelton
Managing Editor: David A. Kirchner
Copy and Production Editors: Marsha Jahns,
Mary Helen Schiltz, Carl Voss, David A. Walsh

Associate Art Directors: Linda Ford Vermie,
Neoma Alt West, Randall Yontz
Assistant Art Directors: Faith Berven,
Harijs Priekulis, Tom Wegner
Senior Graphic Designers: Alisann Dixon,
Lynda Haupert, Lyne Neymeyer
Graphic Designers: Mike Burns, Mike Eagleton,
Deb Miner, Stan Sams, Darla Whipple-Frain

Vice President, Editorial Director: Doris Eby
Group Editorial Services Director: Duane L. Gregg

Senior Vice President, General Manager: Fred Stines
Director of Publishing: Robert B. Nelson
Vice President, Retail Marketing: Jamie Martin
Vice President, Direct Marketing: Arthur Heydendael

All About Your House: Outside Your House
Project Editor: James A. Hufnagel
Associate Editors: Leonore A. Levy, Willa Rosenblatt Speiser
Copy and Production Editor: Carl Voss
Building and Remodeling Editor: Joan McCloskey
Furnishings and Design Editor: Shirley Van Zante
Garden Editor: Douglas A. Jimerson
Money Management and Features Editor: Margaret Daly

Associate Art Director: Linda Ford Vermie
Graphic Designer: Mike Eagleton
Electronic Text Processor: Donna Russell

Contributing Editors: Stephen Mead and Jill Abeloe Mead
Contributing Writers: Robert Dickelman, Leonore A. Levy,
Mary Helen Schiltz, Willa Rosenblatt Speiser, Marcia Spires,
Peter J. Stephano

Special thanks to Sharon Haven, William N. Hopkins,
Bill Hopkins, Jr., Babs Klein, and Don Wipperman
for their valuable contributions to this book.

INTRODUCTION

The outside of your house does several important jobs. First and foremost, it puts a roof over your head, wraps walls around you, and shelters your family from the vicissitudes of nature. Second, your home's exterior makes a visual statement to the world, much as do the clothes you wear and the way you groom yourself. Finally, the outsides of most houses also provide cover (or at least parking) for the family wheels, and a deck, patio, or porch for outdoor living.

Outside Your House delves into each of these roles. It tells how rain, wind, ice, snow, and sunlight punish roofing, siding, and other exterior surfaces. You'll learn how to identify maintenance needs and attend to them before they turn into costly major repair projects, how to select materials that can reduce maintenance chores, and how to go about replacing roofing and siding.

A well-maintained house is a well-groomed house, but what if you're not entirely pleased with the way your home looks, even at its best? If that's your dilemma, *Outside Your House* can help you plan a change of face.

More than two dozen photographs and drawings present the basics of exterior design and color scheming; dozens more offer styling ideas you can adapt.

Caring for the outside of your house can pay big dividends in the long run. So can maintaining your family's car or cars. In fact, if you add up the prices of all the automobiles you'll buy in a lifetime, you may discover that the total approaches the market value of your home. Clearly, it makes sense to plan protection for the cars at your house. An entire chapter tells how.

Outside Your House doesn't neglect outdoor living, either. Nearly 40 pages show and tell how to pull off projects ranging from expanding a small stoop to a whole-yard development scheme that pushes outdoor living to the lot lines.

Join us for a stroll around the outside of your house. If you like our ideas and advice, you may want to look into other volumes of the Better Homes and Gardens ALL ABOUT YOUR HOUSE Library. This comprehensive series of books explores just about every area and element of a modern-day house.

CONTENTS

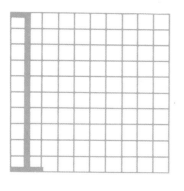

EVALUATING THE OUTSIDE OF YOUR HOME

When you're driving through an unfamiliar neighborhood, you probably notice many things about the homes you pass—their materials, their color schemes, how well they're maintained, and how they're landscaped. Now analyze the outside of your own house as if you were passing by for the first time. Do you like it? Does something seem to be lacking? Could your home's exterior and its surroundings be improved upon? This chapter points out some of the main areas to consider when you're evaluating what could, should, or must be done to improve your home's looks and livability.

COULD YOUR HOME BENEFIT FROM A FRESH NEW LOOK?

It took an entirely new paint scheme, major landscaping changes, and lots of imagination to transform a boring little house into the attention-getting cottage pictured here. Originally the house was painted plain-Jane white, with no contrasting trim. Landscaping consisted mainly of a sun-baked lawn and a concrete patio. The owners turned it into a cheerful home with an imaginative paint job. Practical and attractive landscaping changes, such as dry-laid brick paths, well-mulched flower beds, and abundant shrubbery, completed the transformation.

Your home's architectural personality may be very different from this one, but when you're considering restyling, the same basic points apply.

First, analyze your home's size, shape, and surface materials. There's not much you can do about size and shape without a major remodeling, but you can do a lot about the surface materials. Next, consider architectural features, such as doors, windows, and trim. Do they look right, or are they somehow out of balance? Would new trim colors make the house more interesting?

Take a look at your landscaping, too. Does the house seem to stand forlornly, without sufficient greenery or other natural decoration? You can't put in an instant forest, of course, but a few plantings can do a lot to dress up your home.

For architectural ideas about improving the overall exterior appearance of your home, see Chapter 2—"Giving Your Home a New Look." For more about choosing the colors that will bring out the best in your home, see Chapter 3—"The Importance of Color." To find out more about new-look landscaping, turn to pages 60-63.

EVALUATING THE OUTSIDE OF YOUR HOME

WOULD YOU LIKE TO REDUCE EXTERIOR MAINTENANCE?

Somebody has to take care of a house and its grounds. Even if you have willing children or professional help, you're probably interested in finding ways to cut down on maintenance chores. No matter what your home's style or age, there are many ways to reduce the amount of time and money you need to spend on keeping up appearances.

The striking Colonial saltbox pictured *at left* looks like a meticulously cared-for period piece. It *is* well cared for, but the process isn't nearly as complicated as the home's appearance suggests.

This house, built less than a decade ago from an original saltbox design, offers several ideas for cutting down on maintenance needs.
• The narrow clapboard siding, perfectly in keeping with the home's style, has been treated with a preservative and left to weather naturally. That means it won't require periodic painting or staining to keep it looking its best.
• The wood-shingled roof, treated with a fire retardant, will last for decades. Repairs on individual shingles can be made quickly and inexpensively as necessary.
• The small-paned windows are double-glazed, so there's no need to put up and take down separate storm windows.
• A broad expanse of lawn provides a gracious setting for this home. Although the lawn does take a substantial amount of time to mow, the job is fairly easy because the land is level and unobstructed—an ideal candidate for a tractor-type mower. Young evergreen foundation plantings, which will frame the house in a few years, also require little care beyond occasional pruning and mulching.
• The gravel turnaround driveway works well with the country look and setting of this house. Because the area is level, gravel presents no problems of drainage or shifting surface; because the climate is a mild one, with only occasional snow, gravel is a good choice for all seasons, though it needs to be replenished every few years.

Maintenance priorities
Most homes call for a certain amount of preventive maintenance. Trim needs to be painted periodically. Established trees and shrubs should be pruned before they become overgrown. Siding, roofing, doors, and windows may require occasional repairs. But with thoughtful upgrading, you can totally eliminate some maintenance miseries.

If your home has badly deteriorated wood siding, for example, you might want to consider replacing it with low-maintenance manufactured or natural wood siding. Keep in mind, though, that if a house is more than 50 or 60 years old or historically significant, changing major exterior components may have a negative value for resale as well as aesthetic reasons.

No matter what the age of your house, some changes are bound to make sense—for example, replacing separate storm and screen windows with combination windows.

Other modifications depend primarily on what you like to do around the house and what you find burdensome. If you enjoy gardening, concentrate on reducing maintenance needs for the house itself; if you aren't especially interested in your yard as long as it looks presentable, consider low-maintenance landscaping, including nonorganic materials.

For more about identifying your home's maintenance needs, see Chapter 6—"Exterior Maintenance"—and Chapter 10—"Tools, Tasks, & Techniques." For more about cutting down on upkeep chores, see Chapter 4—"Creating a Low-Maintenance Exterior."

HOW COULD NEW CLADDINGS CHANGE YOUR HOME'S APPEARANCE?

Siding and roofing materials have almost as much to do with the way a house looks as its shape and setting do. Claddings also largely determine your home's exterior maintenance needs. New coverings are costly—you probably wouldn't reroof or re-side purely on an aesthetic whim. If, however, you've recently purchased a house in need of new surface materials, or own one whose roof or siding is wearing thin, by all means consider appearance as well as practicality.

Claddings are made to last, but not all live forever. Brick and stone can endure for centuries; shingles, stucco, clapboard, and other materials, such as many manufactured sidings, have shorter life expectancies.

If your siding is coming to the end of its usefulness and attractiveness, what would happen to your home's appearance if you changed to a different material? If a change would be an improvement, you might want to do something as dramatic as the siding replacement pictured *at right*. The owners chose to strip off the old white asbestos shingles that covered the main part of the house, along with the brick veneer that covered the foundation. To give the house a less awkwardly vertical appearance, they opted to install new redwood siding and frame the windows and first and second stories with wide white trim boards. To minimize the impact of the downspouts, the owners rerouted them behind the new siding.

Although new roofing offers fewer design options than siding does, keep in mind the importance of both color and material. If you are replacing a wood or manufactured shingle roof, you'll probably stay with the original materials; you may not have that option if the original roof is tile or slate. And even if you use the same material, color can make a big difference. For example, replacing black asphalt shingles with medium-brown or charcoal-gray tones could improve your home's color scheme, or spark an entirely new one.

For more about roofing and siding materials, see Chapter 7—"Selecting & Installing Claddings." For another example of how re-siding changes a home's appearance, see pages 26 and 27.

EVALUATING THE OUTSIDE OF YOUR HOME

DO YOU NEED MORE PRIVACY?

Wide-open spaces can be too much of a good thing. Pleasant as it may be to sit on a front porch and visit with passersby, or barbecue in the backyard and wave to your neighbors, there are times when nothing is more appealing than to lie back on a chaise, close your eyes, and hear only birds and rustling leaves. Privacy has more practical aspects, too. If you have a pool, for example, a fence may be a legal requirement. And if you do a lot of outdoor entertaining, a hedge may be necessary to keep the conversation in your outdoor living area from disturbing your neighbors.

The patio and deck pictured *at right* are nestled behind a suburban home with close-in neighbors on all sides. Thanks to the combination of an angled fence and dense greenery, the 25x40-foot space is as private as a large estate. (For more about this yard and the patio that gives it much of its personality, see pages 136 and 137.)

As this photograph shows, privacy needn't depend entirely on a solid fence. Here, established trees and shrubs do part of the job. Other, less common natural privacy "fences" are hills and berms.

A berm is simply a mound of soil, three or four feet high. Placed between a house and street, it can add visual interest to your lot, reduce noise, and block much of the view from the street. Unlike berms, hills aren't something you can add on your own. If your home is on a hilly site, however, planting just a few shrubs and fast-growing trees in strategic locations can do wonders. Because the hill already blocks part of the view to or from the outside world, a little additional landscaping can add more privacy than you might expect.

If your yard has no natural privacy-creating features, several options are available. A fence is the easiest, but it needs careful planning to be attractive and avoid giving your yard a boxed-in look.

Shrubs can be excellent sources of almost-instant privacy. A thick hedge not only blocks unwanted views, it can muffle noise as well. Garden centers often sell shrubs that are tall enough to provide some privacy the first year they're planted.

For more about creating outdoor privacy in your outdoor living areas, see pages 130–133 and 140–141.

WOULD YOU LIKE TO CUT DOWN ON YARD WORK?

Instead of relaxing, do you spend weekends caring for your yard—or feeling guilty because you're not? In either case, analyze your outdoor obligations with an eye toward scaling them down. If you'd rather not keep pace with the cycle of feeding, weeding, watering, and mowing that nurtures a large picture-perfect lawn, plan a landscape that reduces lawn area. Ground covers, for example, require almost no care once they're established. Or consider decks, patios, porches, gazebos, and other man-made structures that can add versatility to outdoor living space while they cut down on lawn area. You also may find that you're spending inordinate amounts of time on yard work because plantings don't suit the soil and light conditions of your lot. Appropriate plantings will make your yard easier to care for and more attractive.

When the owners of the suburban cottage pictured *above* remodeled their home's exterior, they included new landscaping in the plan. Because large trees shade the front of the property, it's difficult to grow grass near the house. In addition, a simple, straight-line concrete pathway added little to the home's approach.

Cedar decks and walkways changed all that, as did shade-tolerant shrubs and perennials that soften the foundation and surround the trees. These plantings require only minimal care, and the remaining lawn has enough light to thrive. See pages 60 and 61 for another view of this property; for information about choosing low-maintenance plants for your yard, turn to pages 62 and 63.

In the backyard shown *at right*, a series of concrete pads laid diagonally makes this narrow lot appear far more spacious than its dimensions. Not only can adults pull up chairs and tables and enjoy the outdoors, the concrete also makes an ideal roadway for children's vehicles and provides a hard surface for bouncing balls and skipping rope. The homeowners can give their now-small lawn all the attention it needs to stay lush and green. Daylilies, ornamental grasses, and other colorful plantings fill in irregular-shaped areas of the yard that would be difficult to mow.

If you'd like to increase the unplanted areas of your yard, turn to Chapter 9—"Improving Outdoor Living."

ARE YOU MAKING THE MOST OF EXISTING OUTDOOR LIVING AREAS?

On the kind of day that entices you outdoors, do your home's outside living areas live up to your expectations? Can you sit comfortably on the back porch, or do you first have to wade through an array of bicycles, flowerpots, and old furniture? Is your patio little more than a blazing patch of concrete? Strategically placed trees, umbrellas, or trellises might be all you need to make it more inviting. In fact, going out, even if it's just outside the door, can be a special occasion if the setting is right.

The idyllic Victorian porch shown *at right* was once a dilapidated eyesore with rotted wood and peeling paint. The floor had to be shored up, and more than half of the balusters were replaced, using one of the originals as a template. New wicker furniture, pots of bright blooms, and country accessories completed the transformation.

If a porch, deck, or patio at your house is in poor repair, your first step should be to make it structurally sound. With that behind you, consider adding amenities to make your outdoor living area more appealing.

Problem-solvers

Flying invaders can send porch sitters scuttling indoors. Screening will keep insects out; and if you select new solar screens, you can deflect heat from your porch as well. With screening in place, add a table and chairs, and perhaps a ceiling fan for cool alfresco dining. In Chapter 8— "Porches, Patios, Decks, and Stoops"—you'll see how other families improved their outdoor living areas.

Do you love the taste of barbecued food, but cook out infrequently to avoid the mess of a charcoal fire? Installing a gas grill on a deck or patio might be the answer. With a gas grill, permanent ceramic briquettes take the place of charcoal, and controls let you regulate the heat, much as you do on a conventional oven.

Finally, if you head indoors when it gets dark, you're missing out on enjoying cool nighttime air. Outdoor lighting might extend your time in the great outdoors. And if your problem is too much daylight, pages 120–121 and 134–135 offer suggestions for shading a patio or deck.

CAN YOU EXPAND OUTDOOR LIVING AREAS?

Perhaps yours is a sloping lot that's lovely to look at but hard to set a chair on. Maybe you've worked so hard on a manicured lawn that children can't play there. Or it could be that your door opens onto nothing more than a concrete stoop that has room for only the newspaper and a welcome mat. If outdoor living space at your house seems inadequate, expanding it can be as simple as pouring a small concrete patio outside the back door, or as ambitious as constructing a multilevel deck that wraps around the entire house.

The cedar deck shown *at left* offers a place to set an inviting breakfast table amidst the greenery of a heavily wooded hillside yard. Before the deck was built, the yard's dense undergrowth made it all but unusable for outdoor living. Designed to follow the contours of a small, odd-shape lot, the deck juts out at a 45-degree angle on one end. Built-in benches and canvas chairs provide plenty of seating in a small area.

A deck can be a simple wooden platform erected at ground level on flat land or a more complex structure raised on sturdy posts to extend over sloping terrain. Turn to pages 122–125 to see a variety of decks and learn about constructing them.

Some decks have humble origins. Even a small deck with a bench can turn a purely transitional stoop into a comfortable seating spot. Pages 126 and 127 show a pair of decks that are built atop old concrete stoops.

A yard-full of possibilities

If your present patio doubles as a speedway for tricycles or as an impromptu ball court, consider expanding the paved areas of your yard to create separate sections for active recreation and quieter pursuits. You might even want to develop your entire backyard into activity centers. Pages 140–145 show a whole-yard development that came about in stages over a period of several years. Pages 128–139 offer a variety of other ideas for expanding the outdoor living at your house.

EVALUATING THE OUTSIDE OF YOUR HOME

DO YOU HAVE ENOUGH SPACE FOR CARS?

Cars are almost considered members of the family, and in multi-vehicle households, finding room for them is a top priority. Neighborhood regulations that prohibit on-street parking can quickly turn a home's yard into an unsightly parking lot. The kind of facilities you plan for cars at your house depends on how many and what type of vehicles you own, drivers' schedules, the climate in your area, and how much space you have.

If you block your front walk when you park, often have to move other vehicles to free yours, or occasionally find tire tracks on the lawn, you probably haven't devoted enough space and thought to accommodating cars at your house.

Start planning improvements by deciding what type of space you need. Do you need a drive wide enough for two cars to pass, or a turnaround to avoid backing into traffic? If this is the case, just a few more feet of paving might be all you need to alleviate the car crunch. You may have to sacrifice part of your lawn, but the return in convenience might be more than worth it.

Paving needn't be unattractive, as you can see in the photo *at right*. Here a wide sweeping driveway provides a turnaround and ample outdoor parking in front of a contemporary ranch house. The architect specified pea gravel, which is practically maintenance free, as are other loose-fill materials. The gravel's soft brown-gray hue blends with the landscape.

For overnight parking, especially in harsh climates, or for storing infrequently driven vehicles, a closed garage protects vehicles from the elements and vandals. If your garage is presently clogged with household overflow, consider freeing up the space with a garage sale, well-planned storage, or both. A large suspended shelf that juts out over the hood of a parked car, for example, makes use of space that would otherwise be wasted.

In mild climates, a carport can make parked cars more unobtrusive and provide shelter from rain and sun. Chapter 5—"Cars at Your House"—tells how to plan driveways, carports, and garages that might be just the ticket for you.

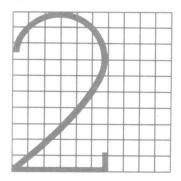

GIVING YOUR HOME A NEW LOOK

The way your home looks to passersby and to neighbors affects the image of your own property and the entire community as well. Certainly a home must be well maintained to even begin to look attractive, but there's much more to an appealing exterior than maintenance. Proportion, materials, details, and style each contribute to the overall impression your home makes. This chapter identifies some of the most notable aspects of exterior design and explores improvements that can add charm and distinction to your home's public appearance.

FIRST, STEP BACK AND TAKE A GOOD LOOK AT YOUR HOUSE

You probably see your house briefly every day, but when did you last take a long, analytical look at it? If you're thinking of changing your home's appearance, your first steps should be to the street, where you can see your house as your guests and neighbors do. Does your house have "curb appeal?"

A large house can appear spacious, or sprawling. A small house can look cozy, or cramped. Much of the difference has to do with the relationships between a home's various features—how they look individually and together, and how they look as part of the entire exterior.

Most of us grew up knowing (or realizing after a few unsuccessful attempts at imitation) that a friend's hairstyle wouldn't necessarily look as good on us. So it is with houses. A bay window that

looks great on a narrow Victorian brownstone may seem awkward on the front of a low-slung ranch; a massive stone chimney that adds strength and charm to a vertical-sided contemporary could make a substantial, squared-off stucco structure look too heavy.

Landscape materials, too, must be in scale with the home they are intended to complement. A pair of evergreens planted in the dooryard a few decades ago may have taken over the whole front yard, obscuring the view from within and overpowering the house as it appears from the street.

When you're considering how the parts of your house fit together, you also need to think about what architects call *mass*. Mass refers to the visual space a home occupies. For example, a center-hall Colonial with living room, dining room, den, kitchen, and powder room on the first floor and four bedrooms and two baths on the second can look quite compact. However, arranging rooms with the same dimension on one floor could take up more visual space, depending on the floor plan.

Scale versus size

This doesn't mean, however, that a single-level house necessarily looks large. The home illustrated *above* shows how exterior elements can balance each other to minimize mass. The house consists of several wings at right angles to each other, each wing almost a small house in itself. When all the pieces are put together, this is a big house, but it doesn't look that way at first, because each major element is moderate in size.

Lesser elements are moderately scaled, too. Note the small-paned double-hung windows used on much of the facade and the small panels on the front and garage doors. But using double doors at the main entry expands the scale here; large-paned windows to the left of the entrance signal that this is a passageway from one zone of the home to another.

Plantings also are moderate in scale, with just a single ornamental tree and low shrubbery in front of the house. In back, tall trees shelter the house from summer sun; tall chimneys add vertical elements to keep the house in scale with its backdrop.

If your home doesn't make as good an impression as you'd like, perhaps you should consider a restyling project. On the following pages are seven examples that introduce you to design basics and present ideas you might adapt.

SOLVING WINDOW PROBLEMS

POOR WINDOW PLACEMENT

Windows, and the way they're arranged, play a major role in defining your home's overall appearance. Do your windows look right? If not, they may be misplaced, mismatched, or of a style that's inappropriate to the rest of the house.

Misplaced windows create a facade that seems out of balance. In most cases, windows should be in vertical and horizontal alignment.

Mismatched windows contribute to a disorganized look. Though not all windows need be exactly the same size or style, they should relate to each other in some way.

Style is to some extent a subjective matter, but beware of designs that seem wildly out of place and from different historical periods. Several different styles of windows can work well together if they're carefully chosen and in keeping with your home's overall design.

A case study

The drawings on these two pages show three versions of a simple, Colonial-style house. It's unlikely that any one house would have as many window-related design problems as the drawing *above* illustrates, but even one or two of these can spoil the appearance of an otherwise attractive home.

The doorway has a decidedly period look, with a pediment, pilasters, and a paneled door; it makes the windows look even more out-of-place than they might with a less-distinctive entry. Only two of the five windows are the same size. The picture window to the right of the door isn't centered on the wall between the door and the end of the house, nor is it aligned with or centered

beneath the second-story window. The middle window on the second floor is centered over the door—a good idea—but that window is too small for its setting.

The drawing *opposite, above* shows how much better the house would look with new, uniformly sized and regularly spaced windows. Colonial in style, these small-paned windows and their simple shutters suit the style of the house.

The drawing *opposite, below* takes a more innovative approach. Here the emphasis is not on Colonial-style detailing but on creating an interesting facade. The original windows were retained, and changes in trim and paint were used to improve the windows' *apparent* proportions. Painted panels

beneath and tall shutters on either side make the undersize windows more prominent. The shutters and panels also serve as unifying features.

On the main level, a new porch minimizes the impact of the picture window and lends a touch of old-fashioned charm. Applying trim to the garage door and painting it in a paned pattern add visual interest. The new frame around that door matches the bracketed angles where the columns of the new porch meet its roof.

Historical highlights

No matter what the style of your home, you can use several types of windows without going wrong, but keep a few points in mind.
• Homes from the Colonial period and the four or five decades immediately following usually had multipaned double-hung windows. Later-vintage homes that approximate earlier styles generally have at least

one sash with small panes, but sometimes the lower sash consists of one large pane.
• Homes in other styles from the late nineteenth and early twentieth centuries often have larger panes, typically only one or two per sash.
• Tudor-style homes usually have casement windows, frequently though not always with small, mullioned panes.
• The classic ranch houses of the 1950s and 1960s have at least some high, horizontal windows; these emphasize the buildings' low-slung lines and may be accented by one or two picture windows.

TWO POSSIBLE ALTERNATIVES

UNIFYING
THE EXTERIOR

Variety is the spice of life, but too much variety can make the exterior of just about any house look disorganized and patched-together. Well-chosen materials used prudently are key factors in creating a unified exterior.

The split-entry home in the photo *opposite* exemplifies the importance of materials in the

success or failure of an exterior. Here, white lap siding on the front contrasts sharply with brick at the front entry and on the end walls and foundation.

This house has another problem, one of scale and proportion: It has horizontal, ranch-house-style windows on walls that are nearly two stories high. In addition, a high,

peaked gable above the entrance disrupts the roofline.

The suggested exterior remodeling illustrated *at right* replaces the lap siding with vertical board siding; 1x4 and 1x12 lumber accents corners and borders. To eliminate the

false-front look, the designer suggests covering the brick with new siding and trim materials that wrap around both sides of the house.

New heavy trim around the lower-level windows creates further unity by visually linking these windows with other portions of the facade. The same treatment for the upper windows, combined with rough-sawn panels below them, brings them into better proportion with the size of the house.

A few other changes complete the transformation. Removing the gable drops the roofline. This gives the house a stronger horizontal emphasis, which is in keeping with its overall style. A fixed-glass sidelight to the right of the front door gives the entry distinction and adds horizontal strength to what was formerly a fragmented-appearing entrance.

ADDING ON CORRECTLY

Sometimes the better your house looks, the harder it is to add on to it. That's because originally the house was so well designed that it simply doesn't need any visual improvement. If, however, you need more room and don't want to move, adding on is a logical course of action.

Scale, style, and materials are among the most important considerations in adding on. It's important, for example, not to dwarf a small house with an obvious and massive addition, or add a distractingly small addition to an otherwise well-proportioned home.

Style and materials needn't match the originals, but they should be compatible. If you have a contemporary wood-sided home, for example, you might decide to add on in an equally modern style, but choose a complementary rather than a matching material.

If your home is traditional in design, you could choose to build an unobtrusive addition in a later style. Or you could carry out the original theme, as shown here.

The Tudor-style brick-and-half-timbered home pictured *above* is well-proportioned and fits well into its setting. The drawing *at right* shows how an addition could be constructed to extend the house at one side without spoiling the balance or lessening the impact of the style. Note how the addition's gable front echoes the taller gable of the original, which in turn is echoed by the front entry gable.

The designer suggests that the new portion of the exterior should be part brick and part half-timbered to match the original home. The new brick must be carefully selected to match the old.

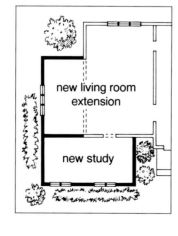

new living room extension

new study

GIVING YOUR HOME A NEW LOOK

RECAPTURING A STYLE

Many older homes no longer look quite as their builders intended them to look. For better or worse, the loss or addition of trim, shutters, doors and windows, porches, or siding can drastically change a home's personality. Some older homes never were a model of the craftsman's art; they had little charm to lose, and it's up to you to add some.

The simple house pictured *above* is typical of many built around the middle of the nineteenth century. With much of its original ornamentation removed, it presents a bland face to the world, with an awkward carport more suitable for a mid-twentieth-century home than one a century older.

The drawing *at right* shows one way to dress up the house. New fretwork at the eaves and above the porch suggests the Gothic Revival style popular during the home's early days. On the roof a custom-made finial heightens the effect, providing a more appropriate accent than the out-of-period American eagle shown in the photo.

Replacing the single-pane sashes with small-pane windows is one way to provide a more historical look, the route that was chosen here. Installing new windows with only two panes per sash would be equally valid. Small panes were still being used at the same time that larger panes were becoming widespread.

New rounded arches over the two large first-floor windows and a new round-topped second-story window are Italianate features. Many homes built around 1850 show the influence of more than one style; using these windows reflects that diversity. For a more consistently Gothic look, use windows with pointed arches.

EMPHASIZING A STYLE

Many homes of recent vintage are built to suggest the style and charm of past centuries. Sometimes, however, the exterior doesn't make as clear a stylistic statement as you might like, especially in these days of renewed interest in our architectural heritage.

The house pictured *above* is generally Colonial in style, but several features detract from its appeal. Stone veneer on the main house and siding on the addition are neither in period nor compatible with each other. The shutters flanking the small-paned windows are too narrow, and the ground-floor shutters extend to the ground, rather than to the top of the exterior sill. At the front entry, double doors are out of both scale and period. Less noticeable, this house is not up to today's energy efficiency standards.

The drawing *at right* shows how an energy-efficient exterior remodeling could strengthen the New England Colonial theme. New, insulated, easy-care lap siding on both the main house and the addition has the narrow-board look of Colonial-era homes. Simulated corner boards and dentil molding help define the style.

Relocating windows creates better balance and allows for more authentically arranged shutters. This may be a more expensive and complex project than you'd like to carry out just for the sake of period accuracy. Keep in mind, however, that installing new, energy-thrifty windows can bring considerable savings in heating and cooling costs.

Putting in a new paneled front door—again, with modern-day energy-saving features—and flanking it with a shatterproof sidelight completes the look.

UPDATING A CONTEMPORARY HOME

covered drive

AFTER

entry terrace

Sometimes a home that seemed to be in the mainstream of architectural tastes for a few decades no longer fits current tastes and life-styles. Many homes built in the 1950s and 1960s, for example, have stark, boxy lines. Although their interiors often are comfortable and well planned, their exteriors may lack warmth and personality and generally look out-of-date. Adding some architectural details, changing surface materials, and creating more effective landscaping are good ways to change all that.

A case study

The home pictured *opposite, far left* has considerable potential, but it also has a bare look, due in part to its very plain surfaces and in part to its lack of foundation landscaping. The drawing *below* shows how the house could be transformed into a distinctive and instantly appealing home.

A new stucco wall extending beyond the garage at left provides better visual balance—the house already has a wing on the right side—and also screens a storage/service area adjacent to the garage. New timbers jutting from the roofline add interesting shadows throughout the day, bringing depth and texture to the home's facade. In a rainy climate, this canopy could be roofed over for additional shelter along the path between the garage and the front entry.

By covering the brick of the central portion of the home with white stucco, the designer creates a stronger focal point. As the drawing and landscape plan *opposite* show, small plants and bushes around the foundation and along the driveway further emphasize the central portion of the house and define the approach to the front door. The plantings used here are suited to a mild, sunny climate, but the same landscaping ideas can be translated to any climate, using species that do well in your region.

CREATING AN ENTIRELY NEW LOOK

The pretty Cape Cod cottage pictured *above* is an example of an American dream that's now a generation past its prime. Although this is an attractive and well-maintained home, the owners wanted a more dramatic, contemporary look.

In analyzing the original design, they found several weaknesses. The one-car garage tucked toward the rear is too small for today's multi-car families and looks awkward in that location. The home's symmetrical facade, combined with its small size, gives it a stodgy and cramped appearance; conservative landscaping reinforces this impression.

Now examine the suggested updating shown *at right.* By adding a post-and-beam carport in front of the garage, the designer not only provides space for a second car but creates a sleek, horizontal line from the lower portion of the extended roof all the way to the outer wall of the new carport. The new roof overhang plays an important role not only here but also across the overall length of the house. In addition to providing shelter from rain and snow, it adds substance and drama to the home's facade. An open-rafter section above the front door keeps the overhang from being too dominant a feature.

By replacing the original Colonial-style paneled front door with a rustic rough-sawn wood door, the designer creates a more casual feeling. A new shingled fence between the front walk and the lawn and a matching shingled privacy wall to the right add to the informal seaside air.

New landscaping enhances the charm of the entire setting. Boulders brought from a nearby hillside and a collection of ground-hugging evergreens add their own appeal and delineate the transition from the driveway to the front path and newly created narrow porch.

AFTER

carport

entry walk

stoop

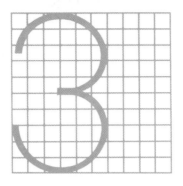

THE IMPORTANCE OF COLOR

From the little red schoolhouse to the White House, the color of a building makes a first and lasting impression. Color can help a home blend in with its natural surroundings or boldly assert its presence as a man-made structure. You can use color to highlight architectural features and show off the proportions of a well-designed home, or visually reshape an awkward house. You can emphasize your home's link to the past with historic colors, or use paint and stain to modernize a dated house. Best of all, you can give your house a fresh new look without seriously denting the family budget. With the wide range of paints and stains available, you'll be able to select colors you'll feel glad to come home to.

COLOR CONSIDERATIONS

You might buy a sweater or tie on impulse because of its wonderful color, but you'll probably devote a great deal of thought to the colors you choose for your home's exterior. It's worth taking time to select a color scheme; you can't hide a poor choice.

Start by thinking about the kinds of colors you feel most comfortable with. Do you prefer cool restful sea colors, warm earth tones, bright clear hues, or restrained neutrals? Do you want your house to present a conservative facade, or would you prefer your home to be a bold expression of your own unique taste and flair? Keeping your general preferences in mind, let these considerations shape your final decision.

• *Architecture.* If your home is an example of a particular period style, history may suggest appropriate color combinations. A Queen Anne, for example, can sport an intricate multicolor scheme that shows off its quirky architectural embellishments; a Georgian Revival is white almost by definition. A contemporary ranch, on the other hand, might benefit from semitransparent wood stains that emphasize its use of natural materials and its strong horizontal lines. Consider, too, your home's proportions. Does the garage, for example, seem out of scale? Painting the garage door the same color as the body of the house, rather than a contrasting color, might be all it takes to bring things into balance.

• *Color givens.* If your house has unpainted or unstained elements such as roofs, masonry, stone, or metal sections, you'll need to take their colors into account when planning your scheme. (More about this on pages 40 and 41.)

• *Landscape and climate.* Is your home surrounded by green lawn year-round or does snow cover the ground for many months? A home that looks bright and cheerful in a warm climate surrounded by tropical foliage might seem garish with an unbroken expanse of white snow for a backdrop. Sometimes the landscape can offer color cues. Would you like, for example, to pick up the colors of rocks from the mountains behind your house, or the hues of a desert sunset? Do you want your home to blend subtly with its natural surroundings, or stand out from them?

• *Neighboring buildings.* Whether you like or dislike the color of the Joneses' house, you'll have to consider it if it's next to your own. In general, you'll want to choose a scheme that doesn't clash with your neighbors'. Some communities, often those concerned with historical preservation, allow only certain exterior colors. Even if covenants don't exist, you may prefer to use colors that help give the entire neighborhood a unified feeling.

You may want to change your home's color scheme, but worry about how a dramatically different color combination will look. Thumb through decorating and architecture publications to see if you can find examples of the scheme you have in mind. Also, take note of the colors that owners of homes similar to yours have chosen. The box *opposite* offers more techniques for previewing a new color scheme.

PLANNING ON PAPER

Paint stores are full of color samples to trigger your imagination, but it's often hard to envision how an entire house will look from the color on a tiny paint chip. In addition, the photograph *above* illustrates one way to try out new color schemes on paper. Start by taking a color picture of your house, and have an enlarged print made. Now cover the photograph with tracing paper and experiment with different color combinations, using colored pencils, crayons, markers, or paint.

If you don't want to start with a photograph, sketch the house on a sheet of heavy paper, then follow the procedure above.

The owners of the white and black Colonial home pictured *at upper left* had enjoyed its tried-and-true color scheme for years, but were now ready to try something more adventurous. In the first tracing paper sketch, they experimented with the idea of a dark house body capped by a light-colored roof—a negative of the original scheme.

In the bottom tracing, you can see a less extreme alternative, with a palette of golds, tans, and grays evolving.

After you've narrowed your color choices, buy small quantities of paint or stain and test them on the house itself. Large expanses of color can look quite different.

WORKING WITH COLOR GIVENS

The owners of the house pictured *at left* started planning their color scheme from the top down. The roof of this modified Cape Cod-style home is especially prominent, so paint colors were chosen to harmonize with the charcoal asphalt shingles. Buttery yellow on the clapboard siding balances the darker shade of the roof; black shutters tie the lower half of the house to the upper story. Glossy white on the window frames keeps them from being overpowered by the dark shutters.

This home features a color scheme in which the body color contrasts with the roof color. An alternate approach would be to choose a tint of the roof color for the house body: in this case a light gray. Or pick up an undertone from the roof, and select a gray-blue, gray-green, or even a gray-pink for the body.

When it's time to repaint your own house, determine the condition of the roof. If it's in good shape, you'll want to select colors for the rest of the house that coordinate with the roof's color. If the roof needs to be replaced, consider changing to a different color when you install new materials. Try to select a roofing color you can live with for a long time, keeping in mind that a new roof will last through many paint jobs.

Other elements to consider

Roofs aren't the only elements that contribute relatively fixed colors to a home's overall color scheme. The hues of brick, stone, weathered wood, and aluminum or vinyl siding also need to be taken into account. Unless they've already been painted, it's usually wise to leave these materials the way they are. Painting would only increase maintenance. Instead, vary the colors of painted areas, such as window frames, shutters, and doors for a change of pace.

The trim colors selected for the elegant home pictured *above* were chosen to enhance the multihued brick exterior. Off-white ties the windows and front door with a key color in the brick; brown framing the door and highlighting fascia and soffits harmonizes with darker tones in the brick and ties the house body to the roof.

EMPHASIZING ARCHITECTURE

B efore their latest paint jobs, you'd probably have passed both of the 1880s homes featured here without a second glance. The one pictured *above* was painted plain white; the one shown *opposite* was covered with dull beige siding.

The owners of the house pictured *above* wanted to show off its handsome proportions and emphasize the delicate gingerbread adorning the porch. To do this, they chose a four-color scheme. Warm tan on the house body provides a backdrop for burnt orange shutters and pale yellow trim. Dark green emphasizes the front door, with panels outlined in orange. The same burnt orange used on the porch floor and front steps makes a welcoming entrance.

Buried treasure

The Victorian shown *opposite* was purchased in derelict condition and brought back to its former glory by new owners. Stripping off the drab asbestos siding, they discovered the original clapboard and fish scale siding underneath. After making repairs to the facade, the owners selected a paint scheme designed to bring out the variations in the siding.

Two shades of gray accent the horizontal and vertical clapboard treatments. A third, darker slate color coats the frames of the long, narrow windows. White trim outlines

the roof and divides the sections of siding. As a final touch, bright pink highlights the entryway and gable peak.

In both of these cases, paint was used to highlight architectural assets. If your home has features you'd like to play down, paint also can help. An ungainly dormer, for example, can be made less prominent by painting it the same color as the roof. Or let an obtrusive garage door fade into the background by painting it the same color as the house itself.

PLANNING A TRADITIONAL COLOR SCHEME

If you're the owner of a traditional home, whether it's an authentic Colonial or modern adaptation, history offers lots of inspiration for exterior color schemes. Old paintings, prints, books, museums, and preservation societies can all acquaint you with authentic old color combinations.

To carry them out, most major paint manufacturers produce lines of historic colors that reproduce the soft hues of the past. If your home has particular historical significance, you may want to research and duplicate its original colors. Otherwise, select a combination of period colors that enhances your home's architecture.

Traditional paint schemes often rely on three colors: one for the house body, another for shutters and trim, and a third accent color to frame doors and windows. For a soft look, choose body and trim hues from the same color family (mustard and olive, for example) and accent them with a neutral white or off-white. To create a bolder facade, sharply contrast body and trim colors (black shutters on a white body, for example) and introduce a lively accent color (perhaps red or blue).

Elegance or rustic charm

The turn-of-the-century Dutch colonial house shown *at right* presides over a large corner plot with a carefully tended lawn and plantings, and its color scheme helps give the home a stately, formal appearance. The owners chose a subdued khaki tone for the body, contrasted with assertive black solid wood shutters that match the roof. Off-white widens window and door openings; the same color outlines the entire house.

The home pictured *above* is a reproduction of one built for a New England minister in 1750. A local artisan carved the broken pediment over the front door, and much of the home's trim work was custom made to keep proportions authentic. Although the owners took great care in selecting trim details, they chose not to highlight them with paint because houses of this period typically presented an unembellished facade. Instead, they stained the trim and the pine clapboard siding a soft barn red that lets some of the wood grain show through. Yellow ocher on all the window frames and muntins brings out these elements and breaks up the monochromatic facade. Cedar shingles, left to weather naturally, cap off the roof.

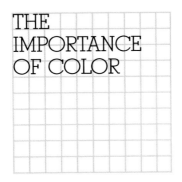

THE IMPORTANCE OF COLOR

COLORING A CONTEMPORARY HOME

Sometimes where you live influences color schemes as much as the type of house you live in. Here the designers of two contemporary homes, one in Connecticut, the other in California, chose dramatically different exterior color schemes.

The home pictured in the inset photograph blends unobtrusively into its woodland setting, and seems to belong there almost as much as the tall oak trees surrounding it. In fact, its color scheme is borrowed from the trees: for the roof, soft green asphalt shingles; for the house body, cedar shakes left to weather to the color of bark.

Wood can be treated with preservatives that protect it from decay but still allow some natural weathering. If you'd prefer not to leave your exterior color scheme up to nature, semitransparent wood stains allow you to add warm color without obscuring the wood's grain.

Western cousin
Thick stucco walls that keep out the heat lend Spanish flavor to the ranch house shown *at right*. Its designer, however abandoned the traditional Spanish-style color scheme of red roof with beige or white stucco walls and instead chose a desert palette touched with a bit of Hollywood. Rose-pink walls, topped by a red tin roof, set a sophisticated yet playful mood. Pale pink outlines window and door openings. Windows and doors appear as cool recesses, thanks to black paint on their frames. Pathways and patios of pink-toned tile carry the house colors to the water's edge. Accents of lavender on a wall and the aqua-blue of the pool keep the facade from becoming monotonous.

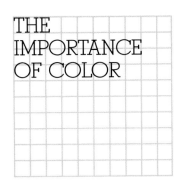

DETAILING DOORS AND WINDOWS

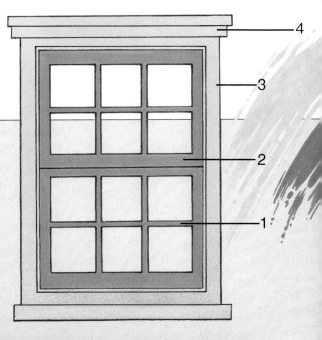

L ike features on a face, doors and windows add character to a home's facade. You can play them up dramatically or accent them subtly depending on the effect you want to achieve. If distinctive framing surrounds your doors and windows, you'll probably want to call attention to it with color, but even standard windows come alive with a well-chosen color scheme.

Outlining windows and doors in white will freshen nearly any color plan. For subtle definition, choose a shade or tint of the main body color.

If you're a bit more adventurous, select a bold accent color to highlight elements of windows and doors. Paint window sashes white, for example, then surround them with barn-red casings or shutters. Or choose a tricolor scheme from within the same color family. Use warm tan on the house body, pale cream on the window frames, and chocolate brown for the shutters.

Even if the rest of your house wears conservative hues, you can highlight the front door with a more dramatic color scheme. In the drawing *opposite,* the traditional-style front door with its broken pediment top and small-paned sidelights could have been painted glossy white. The attractive architecture, however, seems to cry out for more detailing. Here, charcoal gray frames the entryway; contrasting white inserts keep the doorway from appearing too dark and massive. Barn red calls attention to the door itself, with orange accenting the recessed panels. It would be risky to add any more color to this entryway or bring out finer details. Too much variety could turn distinguished detailing into disorganized and distracting elements.

HIGHLIGHTING WINDOWS

When painting windows, follow the numbered sequence on the drawing *at upper right,* starting with muntins and progressing to sashes, casing, lintel, and sill. Here, a dark gray sash is surrounded by a paler gray frame. To bring out more detailing, you could paint the sashes white, the frames dark gray, and the lintels and sill pale gray. Or add punch to the scheme by painting one of the window elements a bright accent color. Use a good-quality sash brush to neatly paint narrow elements. If your hand is unsteady, use a paint shield or apply masking tape on the edges of the panes.

HIGHLIGHTING DOORS

As with windows, paint doors from the inside out, following the numbered sequence on the illustration *at right.* Here the main body of the door and its casing are both dark brown. Thin bands of gold and medium brown outline each recessed panel. For further definition, medium brown also separates the door from its casing.

Alkyd paint is usually the first choice for doors; it provides a durable high-gloss finish that's easy to clean. Mini rollers and foam pads speed painting of narrow door elements.

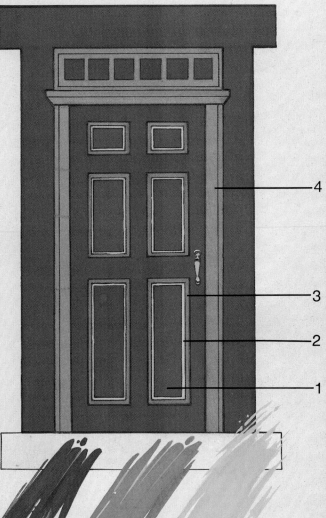

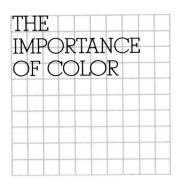

CHOOSING AND USING PAINTS AND STAINS

Once you've worked out a color scheme for your house, you're ready to select specific paints or stains to carry it out. Most coatings come in many colors, so you should be able to execute the scheme you want no matter which type you choose.

Professional house painters tend to favor a particular type and brand of coating; if you'll be doing the job yourself you'll need to decide whether to use a water-thinned *latex* paint or a solvent-thinned *alkyd* paint.

• *Latex* is especially popular with amateur house painters. Brushes and other tools and drips clean up easily with soap and water. Latex paint dries quickly, has excellent color retention, and resists peeling and blistering. (*Acrylic,* a type of latex paint, dries especially quickly.) Latex can be applied successfully to damp, but not wet, surfaces. Because it "breathes," allowing some moisture to pass through it, latex is a good choice if you live in a damp climate or your house has interior moisture problems.

• *Alkyd* paints feature a synthetic resin base that has replaced the oil base used in older formulas. You'll need solvents for cleanup. Alkyd takes longer to dry than latex, but forms an exceptionally durable surface. You must apply alkyd paint to an absolutely dry surface. Because of its excellent hiding power, alkyd works well on woods such as cedar and redwood, which tend to bleed.

Some white alkyds are formulated to *chalk.* These paints self-clean by forming a powdery surface when they dry. With each rainfall, dirt is carried away along with some of the powdered paint. If painted areas are above masonry, don't select a chalking paint; it will stain the masonry below.

If you'll be painting a surface for the first time, select the type of coating that seems most appropriate. With previously painted surfaces, however, you'll usually be better off to continue with the same type of coating. Old latex beneath a new coat of alkyd lets moisture pass through, causing the alkyd to peel. Latex may not adhere properly over a chalking alkyd surface.

Selecting a sheen

Both latex and alkyd paints come in a variety of lusters. Most people prefer a flat finish for large expanses and glossier surfaces for trim and elements that must withstand a lot of handling, such as windows and doors. Trim paints (sometimes called enamels) are available in either semigloss or gloss. Alkyd glosses dry to the shiniest surface, but lose their gloss faster than latex.

When comparing similar types of paints, read the ingredient labels. The more pigment, the better coverage per gallon; the more vehicle, the better adhesion and durability.

One-coat house paints are especially thick and have more resins and pigments than ordinary exterior paints. They are consequently more costly, but can be worth their price in saved application time.

Selecting stains

Instead of hiding wood beneath an opaque coating the way paint does, stains let wood's natural grain show through. Like paints, stains are available in latex and alkyd varieties. Latex stains retain their colors well, and work best on surfaces that are resistant to water. If the surface is too porous, latex's water base can raise the wood's grain and mar a smooth finish. Alkyds penetrate wood to prevent

cracking, and are best suited for use on porous woods.

Stains vary in their degree of coverage. Totally clear coatings are available, but are not recommended because the sun's ultraviolet rays deteriorate them. If you want to protect wood but retain a natural appearance, use a *wood preservative,* which helps resist moisture, decay, fungus, insects, and warping.

• *Semitransparent stains* (sometimes called *penetrating stains*) alter the wood's natural color without obscuring its grain.

• *Solid-color stains* (sometimes called *opaque stains*) provide greater coverage, although some of the wood grain remains visible. This type of stain works well on lower grades of plywood or on blemished surfaces.

• *Bleaching or weathering stains* turn wood a silver-gray color without waiting for nature to weather the raw wood.

If you're painting or staining wood for the first time, or changing to a different type of coating, you'll need to use an appropriate primer or sealer first. The manufacturer's label on the coating you choose will specify the proper primer.

Before you pick up a paintbrush, you'll inevitably need to do a certain amount of preparation. Pages 86 and 87 describe how to prepare a house for painting and how to identify and remedy a variety of paint problems. Additives can be added to ordinary house paints to help them resist environmental problems such as mildew, industrial pollutants, insects, and intense sunlight. If you'll be painting surfaces other than wood, the chart *opposite, top* explains which coatings to chose and how much work is involved in applying them.

Deciding how much to buy

Buying paint isn't an exact science; exactly how much you'll need depends on the condition, type, and porosity of the surface to be covered. A gallon of paint usually covers about 400 to 550 square feet; stains coat less. Labels will give you the manufacturer's estimate of coverage, and dealers often can give you further advice about specific products. If you're repainting with a very similar color, one coat should suffice. Changing colors or covering surfaces for the first time requires two.

To estimate *body paint,* measure from the foundation to the roof overhang and multiply this number by the distance around the house. For a gable, you'll need to figure the area of a triangle. Measure the distance from the overhang to the peak and the width of the wall at the gable's base. Multiply these figures and divide the result by two. Also include the area of soffits if you plan to paint them. Divide totals by the number of square feet covered by a gallon of coating to find out how much to purchase.

Estimate 35 square feet of trim for each window. For gutters, multiply the width times the height times two; for railings, multiply the width times the height times four.

Add an extra 10 percent to your final totals. Standard colors can be returned unopened; custom colors can't. Be sure to save some extra paint for touchups.

Invest in good-quality painting tools; they'll make application easier and faster, and ensure better results. The box opposite will help you choose appropriate implements.

FINISHES FOR SPECIAL SURFACES

MATERIAL	SPECIALTY COATINGS	APPLICATION
PORCHES AND DECKS	These surfaces require exceptionally durable coatings. Choices include alkyd, epoxy, latex, polyurethane, and rubber-base types. Most can be applied to wood or concrete and will dry quickly. Surface preparation varies; read labels carefully.	With most, you pour the coating onto the floor, then spread it out with a long-handled roller or wax applicator.
METAL	Prime bare metal before painting unless you select a rust-inhibiting topcoat. Most metal primers and paints have an alkyd or oil base (although some latex paints can be used over properly primed metal) and include rust-inhibiting ingredients. Select primers and paints that suit the metal you plan to coat.	Metal coatings can be brushed, rolled, or sprayed on. A painter's mitt can help you coat rounded surfaces, such as railings.
MASONRY	Coatings include latex, alkyd, epoxy, portland cement powder, and rubber. Use filler to create a smooth base surface; to reduce porosity, prime with a recommended sealer or select a self-priming paint. Make sure the coating you choose is alkali-resistant.	Latex is easy to apply. Some of the others can be quite difficult.
SIDING ABOVE MASONRY	Some house paints produce a fine surface powder that helps clean the surface when it rains. Chalking paint above masonry, however, can run onto the masonry and cause an unsightly white residue. Select only non-chalking paints.	If siding has previously been coated with chalking paint, thoroughly wash it before painting; use a wire brush for scrubbing old paint from masonry.

BRUSHES, PADS, AND ROLLERS

Select painting implements according to the surface you'll be coating and the type of paint you'll be using. Brushes come in a variety of sizes and shapes, but the three pictured *below* will get you through most jobs. To paint broad surfaces such as siding, try a 4" *wall brush*. A 2" *angular sash brush* and a 2" *flat trim brush* work well on narrow elements and in tight places.

Hog's hair bristles are the first choice for alkyd- or oil-base coatings, varnishes, and shellacs. Do not use them with latex. Nylon or polyester bristles can be used with any coating.

Pads were designed for painting shakes and shingles, and also work on smooth surfaces.

Rollers coat flat surfaces quickly. For smooth surfaces use a short-nap cover; for textured surfaces, a longer nap. Synthetic covers work with any type of paint; use lamb's wool covers only with alkyd- or oil-base coatings.

angular sash / trim brush

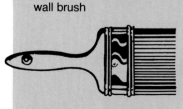

wall brush

flat sash / trim brush

handle may adjust

allows pad removal

frame

foam

fibers — adhesive

core

cover (pile or nap)

bird cage roller frame

grip or handle

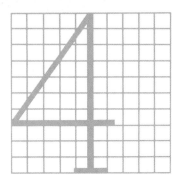

CREATING A LOW-MAINTENANCE EXTERIOR

If you feel as though you're spending too much time maintaining your home's exterior and grounds, you're probably eager to find some things you can do to cut down upkeep. In this chapter, we'll help you analyze the regular exterior maintenance chores required around your house, identify several high-maintenance traps that can make you a slave to the outside of your house, and suggest alternative ways to achieve the best possible results with the least possible toil.

DECIDING WHAT TO CHANGE

The first step toward creating a labor- and time-saving exterior is to take a good look around the outside of your home. Bring along pencil and paper and make a list of regular outside maintenance projects that beckon for your attention, either seasonally, annually, or every two to five years. Note, too, how much time you spend on each project.

Listed below are some high-maintenance areas that require particular scrutiny.
• *Siding.* Is paint peeling? Has siding buckled? Is it loose? Does it need to be caulked? If your home has a brick or stone exterior, are the mortar joints intact, or do they need tuck-pointing?
• *Roof.* Are any shingles loose? Are the shingles in good condition? Is the flashing intact, or showing signs of deterioration?
• *Gutters.* Do they need painting? Are they securely fastened to the fascia? Are they free of debris? Do seams leak?
• *Windows and doors.* Do they need repainting or restaining? Does caulking or glazing compound need to be replaced? Is weather stripping in place?
• *Walks and driveway.* Are surfaces deteriorating or settling? Is grass growing in cracks and over edges?
• *Landscaping.* Do you have more lawn than you care to mow? Are your flowers, trees, or shrubs too much work in the spring and fall?

Setting priorities
If you're an experienced homeowner, you probably already know what you like and dislike about maintaining the outside of your home. If you're unsure about what's involved in certain maintenance chores, turn to Chapter 6 for specifics.

You may enjoy some projects on your list, or even consider them hobbies. If you find certain activities, such as growing flowers or vegetables, relaxing, turn your attention to ways that you can make other, not-so-pleasant jobs less of a chore.

Now you're ready to decide what changes you'd like to make. You'll probably choose to correct the most troublesome maintenance headaches first. Research all your low-maintenance options carefully by learning what materials are available, visiting lumberyards and nurseries, and talking to an architect. Then determine how each change will affect the overall appearance of your house.

Some low-upkeep alternatives may not be good choices for your home because they won't complement its style or aren't suitable for your climate. Some roofing materials may be too heavy for the original frame of your house.

Cost may be a determining factor, too. Low-maintenance alternatives can be costly. If you're planning to move in a few years, you may be better off to invest in a good paint job, for example, rather than cover your entire house with top-quality manufactured siding.

The exterior of the ranch house pictured *opposite* exemplifies maintenance-wise planning. Moderately priced, natural-looking board-and-batten siding requires minimal upkeep. Low-maintenance container plants add a bright finishing touch to the entry, are easily moved, cared for, and replaced, and can be purchased preplanted in pots.

A LOW-UPKEEP
FACE-LIFT

Turning a high-mainte-
nance exterior into one
that requires minimal up-
keep takes planning, but it's
well worth the effort. The owners of the former "handyman
special" shown *above* began
with an overall plan for creating a low-maintenance exterior
and, at the same time, an outdoor living area for relaxing
and entertaining. After some
research and thought, they decided to landscape the large
yard behind the house into a
functional, low-upkeep space
the whole family could enjoy.

The house originally had a
stucco-coated concrete block
exterior. To modernize it, the
owners wrapped the house in
rough-sawn cedar plywood
siding, as shown *at left*. A penetrating oil-base stain was
applied for a low-maintenance
finish that could be expected
to last five to nine years.

New asphalt shingles, metal
flashings, and a vinyl gutter
system were installed to minimize future roof maintenance.
To eliminate the need for storm
windows (and the upkeep that

goes with them), the owners
replaced the original windows
with double-glazed casement
units.

The owners knew from the
outset that they didn't want to
spend their leisure time maintaining a large lawn. So they
reduced the amount of lawn to
mow and created the outdoor
living area they wanted by
building a large deck at the
rear of the house between the
kitchen and bedroom wings. A
smaller deck was built off patio
doors leading to the kitchen.
To avoid future bouts with a
paintbrush, both decks were
constructed from treated fir
and allowed to gray naturally.

Several landscaping materials and techniques also reduced the size of the lawn and
minimized yard work. Beds of
decorative rock mulch and
lawn edgings arranged around
the foundation help control
weeds. Small, slow-growing
shrubs replaced the overgrown
bushes and reduced the risk
of root damage to the home's
foundation. Easy-care container plants, changed with the
seasons, add colorful accents
to the home's exterior. (For
more about planning low-
maintenance landscaping, see
pages 60–63.)

LASTING SOLUTIONS TO MAINTENANCE PROBLEMS

MAINTENANCE SOLUTIONS

PROBLEM

FLASHING

Water seeping under roofing material because flashing has pulled away from the roof surface, roof cement or caulk has dried up, or flashing has rusted out, cracked, or corroded over the years.

ROOF EDGE

Water may not be running off the roof properly. This can result in moisture backing up under the shingles and running down the fascia. If roof shingles are curled, this is probably the explanation.

GUTTERS

A gutter joint may have collapsed, a galvanized or sheet metal gutter may have rusted out, a wood gutter may have rotted, or, if there is an ineffective drip edge, the fascia may have deteriorated so a fascia bracket holding the gutter is not secure.

SOFFIT DAMAGE

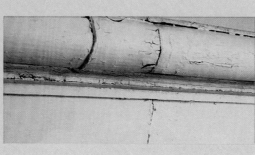

Caused by exposure to excessive moisture due to condensation in under-eave spaces above the soffit or water running off the roof and backing up through a faulty drip edge or gutter.

QUICK-FIX SOLUTION	LONG-TERM SOLUTION	COST/DIFFICULTY
Apply new cement or caulk. Rusted, cracked, or corroded flashings around chimneys, dormers, and plumbing vents will last a few years longer if you trowel on a coat of fibered asphalt-aluminum roof paint.	If widespread deterioration has occurred, replace the flashings entirely, using the same type of material; then reroof around the flashings. Rubber, plastic, and copper flashings require little maintenance.	Aluminum flashing is the least expensive. It's not difficult to replace chimney flashing, but for an entire roof's worth of flashing, you may prefer a professional installation.
Check the drip edge. If there isn't one, or there is but it's rusted, put in a new one. Use an aluminum or galvanized drip edge for asphalt roofs. Repair or replace damaged shingles at this time.	If the roof sheathing and rafter tails are rotting, put on new sheathing, new roofing where damage has occurred, and a new drip edge.	Depends on damage and replacement needs. Installing new sheathing is the most expensive aspect of the procedure.
Replace only the part of the gutter that is deteriorating; use material that is the same as the original gutter. Be aware that other parts of the gutter may collapse or need repair in the future. If a rotting fascia is the problem, install a new drip edge and replace fascia; paint to match.	Install an entire new gutter system. Vinyl gutters impregnated with color throughout the material never need painting.	Aluminum gutters are moderately priced and last 15 to 20 years; vinyl has a lifetime guarantee but is expensive. Installing an entire system is not a do-it-yourself job for most people, but preformed components put it in the "possible" category.
Check where moisture is coming from. If the roof's drip edge or gutters are defective, repair. If wooden soffit structure has not deteriorated, scrape off peeling paint, let the wood dry out, and repaint. If moisture is coming from condensation caused by poor ventilation, install one or more soffit vents.	Install perforated metal or vinyl soffits for maintenance-free upkeep and excellent ventilation.	A manufactured soffit is the most expensive, most effective solution. You can install manufactured soffits to match manufactured siding when you re-side your house.

LASTING SOLUTIONS TO MAINTENANCE PROBLEMS

(continued)

MAINTENANCE SOLUTIONS

PROBLEM

SIDING

Cracks, dents, or decay from age; popped nails in siding; siding pulling away from house; siding deteriorating from exposure to moisture.

PEELING PAINT

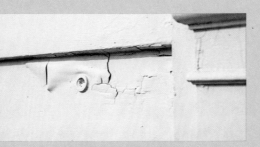

Caused by moisture escaping through the wall from the inside out, prolonged periods of exposure to rain or other moisture, or applying the finish coat of paint or stain over a wet or "green" surface.

SPALLING BRICK

The face of the brick is crumbling or pieces are popping out because of moisture in the brick wall or the house settling.

WINDOW JAMBS, SILLS, & HEADS

Finish is checking, crazing, and peeling from exposure to moisture and sunlight. Wood becomes vulnerable to insects.

QUICK-FIX SOLUTION	LONG-TERM SOLUTION	COST/DIFFICULTY
If popped nails are the problem, pull nails and renail in another spot. Fill holes and finish to match. If the siding is pulling away, the sheathing underneath is probably deteriorating. Take siding off, replace the sheathing, then replace siding. Finish to match. If siding is deteriorating because of a defective downspout, repair the downspout and replace the siding section; finish to match.	Re-side the entire house with vinyl, aluminum, or hardboard siding.	Depends on the quality and type of materials chosen to patch or replace siding. In general, hardboard is the least expensive, vinyl the most costly. Manufactured sidings are only moderately difficult to install. To learn how, see pages 106–109.The warranties on some manufactured sidings may be voided if you do the work yourself.
If siding was wet or green when it was painted, remove the paint, let the siding dry, prime, and paint again. If a leaky gutter is allowing water to run down the siding, repair the gutter, re-side the area, and finish it to match the rest of the house. Or use an exterior primer-sealer; be sure you also have an interior vapor barrier, or moisture from inside the house could be trapped in the wall cavities. Soffit or siding vents may be installed to ventilate the wall cavity.	Select a siding that has a vapor barrier as an integral part of its construction; or remove siding and install a vapor barrier to keep the moisture from penetrating the outside walls, then re-side the entire exterior with vinyl, aluminum, or hardboard.	Installing a vapor barrier and re-siding with a low-maintenance material is an expensive but long-lasting solution. Installing board siding requires extensive carpentry and precise calculations; manufactured siding is relatively easy to install if you follow the manufacturer's instructions to the letter. Leave the job of adding insulation and an interior vapor barrier to a professional.
Behind the brick is a shallow cavity designed to vent moisture into the attic. Check this from the attic or by removing a soffit (you may need a mirror and flashlight). If the passage is blocked and not venting properly, unblock the passage to minimize moisture buildup. If spalling brick results from settling, replace the bricks themselves.	If moisture is freezing and thawing in the bricks, causing part of the brick to dislodge, seal the brick on the outside with a clear spray.	Spraying the brick is inexpensive and easy. Replacing the brick is more expensive and more difficult, requiring some masonry skills.
Cover the affected areas by fashioning metal capping, or replace the parts of the window unit that are damaged by cutting out the sections and fashioning new wood pieces.	If damage is severe, replace the entire window unit.	Protecting parts of the window with metal capping is the easiest and least expensive option. Replacing the entire window is the most costly.

EASY-CARE
LANDSCAPING

The landscape materials you choose for your yard will determine how much or how little upkeep the yard will require. The owners of the house pictured *at right* mixed both growing and nongrowing landscape materials to create a contemporary exterior that combines good looks with minimal maintenance needs.

Originally this 1940s cottage was overhung by mature trees and had overgrown foundation shrubs, an extensive front lawn, and a concrete walk leading to the house. The owners reduced the size of the front lawn by adding a window-walled bump-out and two main decks (made of rot-resistant cedar) to the front of the house. Low-maintenance natural cedar siding replaced the original stucco exterior.

To complement the rustic-looking decks, an easy-care walkway, made by spiking together weather-resistant 4x6 pine timbers, replaced the old walk. Pine boxes constructed from the same treated pine timbers were used to tie together the tree, decks, light posts, and walkway.

The owners chose to keep most of the trees, so the yard does not get abundant light. To add color, they selected hardy shrubs and low-growing perennials that could thrive in the shade. Shade-loving annuals in planters around the trees and in clay pots on the deck provide further highlights.

To learn about landscaping materials that can reduce yard work at your house, turn the page. *(continued)*

EASY-CARE LANDSCAPING
(continued)

You don't have to give up the creative pleasures of gardening for the sake of minimizing maintenance. Once properly planted, many species thrive with little attention. Here are some points to keep in mind.

• Bulbs and perennials are good low-maintenance plants once they are established.

• Avoid shrubs that require frequent pruning.

• Buy trees that don't drop lots of leaves, needles, bark, seeds, flowers, or fruit, and beware of trees that are easily damaged by heavy wind and rain.

Ground rules

Be sure the flowers or shrubs you choose are suited to the area you want to plant them in. Some plants thrive under conditions that would stunt other species.

How and where you plant your flowers, shrubs, or trees will affect the time you spend in the yard in other ways, too. For example, using a gravel or wood-chip mulch around a plant or in a bed of plants helps the soil retain moisture (thereby reducing the need to water) and keeps weeding, edging, and trimming chores to a minimum. A sheet of 6-mil polyethylene under the mulch eliminates weeding altogether. You can reduce edging chores by surrounding plants or beds with aluminum or plastic strips, curbs of brick, railroad ties or landscape timbers. For easier lawn mowing, lay concrete edging strips or pieces of flagstone flush with the soil around fences, lampposts, and other obstructions.

WEEDY PATCHES

Weeds pop up everywhere, even in the most unlikely places, and they present time-consuming maintenance problems. If they're allowed to stay, weeds compete with other plants for food and water, and provide a home for insects. If they're allowed to grow and multiply, they cut down air circulation, creating a disease-ridden environment for nearby healthy plants. The once-weedy patch in the photo *above* was brought under control by first pulling the weeds out by their roots. Then a hardy ground cover called buttercup, a perennial that creeps along the ground by runners, was planted over part of the area. A wood-chip walkway and a low-maintenance wooden deck were built over the rest of the area, creating an easy-care outdoor living area. If you have a weedy patch, use growing and nongrowing landscape materials—and a little imagination—to replace a patch of weeds and create a delightful area in your yard.

BARE FOUNDATIONS

If only grass decorates your foundation wall, save time trimming the grass that the mower can't reach and add interest to your house's exterior by building a mulched bed of plantings, as shown *above*. Select small-growing plants or larger varieties, depending on the style of your house and whether the plantings will be near windows. Add flowering vines to soften an exposed exterior and provide an attractive backdrop for other plants. Edge the bed to help contain the mulch, make mowing the surrounding grass easier, and keep grass from growing into the bed. If your eaves have wide overhangs, be careful not to position plants too close to the foundation—the overhangs will keep rain from falling on the plants. In addition, if the plants aren't given room to grow, roots may damage the foundation. If you're planting large shrubs or lots of shrubs, consider putting a strip of paving along the foundation for easy access to windows and walls.

SLOPES

Slopes are no place for grass. Not only are slopes hard to mow, but grass alone does not adequately stop erosion. In the photo *above,* a path was carved and railroad ties positioned to hold topsoil and make the steeply sloped backyard accessible. Soil-binding ground covers of needlepoint ivy, cinquefoil, and Indian mock strawberries add texture and color to the landscape. These ground covers spread fast and are practically maintenance-free once they're established. For a different look, intersperse trees, shrubs, and large rocks in the ground cover. While you're waiting for ground coverings and other permanent plantings to mature, fill in bare spots with colorful annuals. Also consider terracing to break up a slope in the yard. If space permits, build a retaining wall and cantilever a deck out over the slope. Or turn the bank into a distinctive rock garden.

OVERGROWN WALKS

Have you ever spent hours pulling weeds and grass from between the cracks of your sidewalk, or pruning shrubs that are growing over the walkway? In the photo *above,* one of these time-consuming chores was eliminated by planting low-growing ground covers along the walk. These varieties were used here to give different colors and textures to the landscape. Edging and a mulched bed of low- and slow-growing plants or a strip of poured concrete also could have been used effectively. The walkway itself was created from flagstone, flat irregular-size pieces of stone, mortared right over an existing concrete path. By using this low-maintenance technique, no cracks remained for weeds and grass to grow into. Similar easy-care walkways can be built out of brick, tile, and precast blocks. If you want grass to grow right up to your sidewalk, be sure the soil is flush with the walk to make mowing easier and eliminate hand trimming.

TOO MUCH LAWN

Whatever its actual size, your lawn is too big if it takes more time than you want to spend to mow, weed, feed, water, and rake it. You can reduce the size of your lawn, or eliminate it altogether, by creating a carefree outdoor living space with rock mulch, precast cement patio blocks, and low-maintenance plants, as shown *above.* Other options include weaving free-form gravel paths through the yard or around beds of easy-care shrubs, bulbs, and perennials, or landscaping a narrow mound of dirt, or *berm,* with wood-chip mulch and easy-care evergreens. Consider accenting your yard with colorful islands of ground cover. Be sure to edge all beds, berms, paths, and islands with mowing strips. If you have a very large lawn, consider turning part of it into a self-maintaining—but tidy—meadow with wildflowers and a meandering path of wood chips. If you don't want your lawn to brown off in hot, dry weather, install an automatic sprinkler system.

SHADY SPOTS

Shade can create interesting light patterns for any landscape, but when an area does not receive enough sunlight, grasses die out, bare spots appear as if worn by traffic, and unsightly mud holes emerge after a rain. Avoid these problems in low-light areas by using mulches, building low-maintenance planters or walkways, or planting only hardy, shade-tolerant plants, such as the low-growing ground cover, sweet woodruff, pictured *above.* Despite deep shade, it grows rapidly and even adds color with small white flowers in late spring. Choose other low-maintenance, shade-loving plants among annuals, perennials, bulbs, vines, evergreens, and deciduous flowering shrubs. Two low-maintenance advantages to shade: Plants require less water and flowers almost always last longer.

TROUBLESOME TREES

Trees can add a lot to a yard—including adding a lot of time and effort spent on it. Some trees are less disease- and insect-resistant than others and need spraying regularly. Others drop their fruit or seeds—or a sticky sap—that must be cleaned up regularly. Branches often need to be pruned to keep them from growing over a roof or into the side of the house. Many of these problems can be solved by selecting the *right* trees for your yard. Know why you are buying a particular tree. The tree shown *above,* for example, adds color to the corner of a wooded area. Do you want the tree to grow 15 feet high or 40 feet? Consider replacing a troublesome tree with a low-maintenance evergreen. If too much shade is the problem, thin the branches to let in more light. If mowing around the trunk is a problem, surround the base with a brick mowing strip or create a bed of low-maintenance plants around the base of several trees. Mulch and edge for easy care.

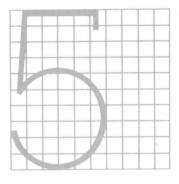

CARS AT YOUR HOUSE

Your family's vehicles deserve a good home, whether that's in the form of open-air off-street parking, a carport, or a spacious multipurpose garage. In this chapter, we'll take a look at designing driveways, planning parking, and getting the right garage—detached or attached—for your needs. Armed with this information, you'll be able to decide whether you can do all or part of the work yourself, or if you'd be better off hiring professionals to handle the entire job.

DRIVEWAY PLANNING BASICS

Compared to the cost of other major home improvements, such as finishing a basement or building an addition, the cost of adding or improving a driveway is relatively low. But the right driveway can have a strong and positive effect on convenience, your home's street appeal, and, ultimately, the home's resale value.

Plan ahead
Careful planning is the key to a good-looking, durable driveway. Start by analyzing how your family functions outdoors, and make a list of all the features you want to incorporate in your driveway project.

Consider how far you'll have to carry groceries from the car to the kitchen. Think about where recreational extras such as a basketball court or tetherball post could go. Look at the possibility of future projects—a garage, backyard barbecue, or patio—that may someday connect to the driveway, and plan now to do the digging for underground plumbing, gas, and electrical lines that will run to those facilities.

The traffic flow near and past your home also affects how well your driveway will work. If you live on a busy street, for example, weigh the advantages of including a turn-around, so you don't have to back into heavy traffic. If your street is lined with "No Parking" signs, consider ways to provide off-street parking for guests.

Now's the time to think about aesthetics, as well. Design a driveway made from materials that will complement your home's exterior and the surrounding landscape. Although concrete or asphalt surfaces conform to almost any situation, they're not the only materials to think about.

You can use a brick driveway, for example, to add a touch of colonial charm, or exposed aggregate to create a rustic look. For more about materials, see pages 66-69.

Rules and regulations
Before you draw up a final plan, visit your local building inspector to make sure your ideas conform to local codes and zoning ordinances. Most communities require that your finished plan be approved before a construction permit is issued. Also check your property deed to be certain your plans fall within building restrictions and appearance standards for your neighborhood.

When you sit down to draw your final plan, use the dimensions from the illustration *opposite* as minimum guidelines. In addition, keep these points in mind:
• The maximum grade should not exceed 14 degrees (about 1¾ inches per running foot). If the grade is greater, cars will scrape the street when entering and exiting the drive. Besides, in cold climates, the combination of a steep grade, snow, and ice can make your driveway hard to negotiate.
• To ensure proper drainage, your driveway should slope about ¼ inch per foot away from your house, garage, or carport. On a level drive you can plan a 1-inch center crown so water will run off to both sides. For a steep or extra-long driveway, include a center gutter—a slightly concave trough that runs the entire length of the pavement to the street or to a drain just in front of the garage.

DRIVEWAYS: NUMBERS TO KNOW

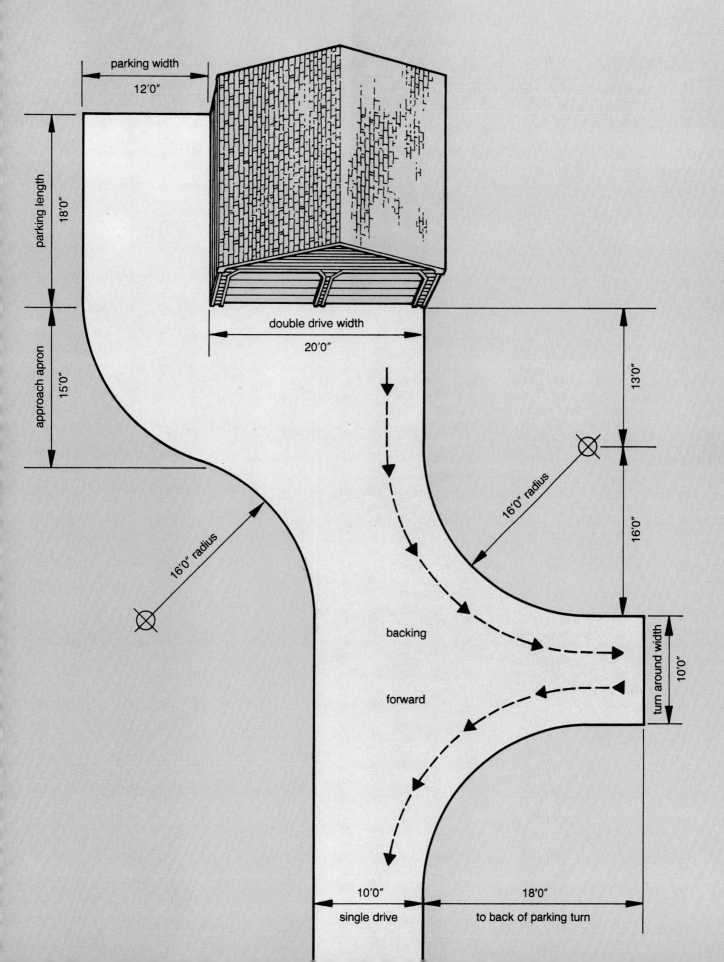

parking width

12'0"

parking length

18'0"

approach apron

15'0"

double drive width

20'0"

13'0"

16'0" radius

16'0"

16'0" radius

backing

forward

turn around width

10'0"

10'0"

single drive

18'0"

to back of parking turn

CARS AT YOUR HOUSE

DRIVEWAY MATERIALS

When you choose the paving material for your driveway, you'll want a good-looking surface that requires minimal upkeep from year to year. Consider, too, how easy your driveway will be to live with from day to day. Is the surface smooth enough so you can easily sweep away grass clippings or shovel snow?

Concrete

Concrete is a tricky building material that has to be worked quickly. Pouring a concrete driveway is no easy task, so you'll probably want to have the job done by professionals.

Concrete forms well into curves, corners, and odd shapes around trees and other obstructions. It also offers a wide range of ways to introduce texture, color, and pattern to your driveway and the overall landscaping scheme of your yard. For example, smooth stones embedded in the exposed aggregate driveway pictured *opposite* suggest a rocky streambed and add interest to the twin tracks.

If you're putting in a completely new driveway, consider how passable it will—or won't—be in icy or snowy conditions. If you live in a cold climate, consider having your concrete contractor bury heating cables in the pavement.

Asphalt

Asphalt is a little more economical than concrete for driveway-size projects. Working with a large expanse of asphalt requires expertise and equipment beyond the reach of most home do-it-yourselfers, however. Don't confuse the "hot-mix" material contractors use for entire driveways with the asphalt-patching compounds sold by the bag in home centers.

The final surface texture of an asphalt driveway depends mainly on the size of the aggregate used by the asphalt supplier. Color usually varies only with age. When first installed, asphalt is a rich, black color; after a few years, it weathers to a medium-to-light gray if it's not resealed with a tar-based coating. Asphalt can be tinted, but you'll probably find the cost prohibitive.

Asphalt has one interesting new virtue. In regions where there's lots of sunshine, some homeowners are using their asphalt driveways as giant solar collectors. Copper tubing buried in the pavement warms water directed to a home's hot water or space heating systems. You also can bury heating cables in asphalt to melt snow and ice.

Loose fill

Requiring less grading and subsurface preparation than concrete or asphalt, a loose-fill driveway is a lower-cost alternative to long-lasting paving materials. And a loose-fill driveway that's been in place for a couple of years makes an excellent base for concrete or asphalt paving.

Depending on where you live, several types of loose fill are available, ranging from crushed limestone to rounded stones such as pea gravel, pebbles, and river rock. Loose fills come in a variety of colors, too, including brown, gray, blue, green, and even white.

The biggest problem with loose-fill materials is that they don't always stay in place. Besides disappearing by the handful when children walk by, loose fill can stick to the tread of car tires, wash away during a rainstorm, or be shoveled away with the snow in winter.

(continued)

DRIVEWAY MATERIALS
(continued)

MATERIALS OPTIONS

| | **SUBSURFACE PREPARATION** | **APPLICATION** |

CONCRETE

Because concrete is very inflexible, a solid subsurface is critical. Remove vegetation and topsoil to the appropriate depth for your driveway thickness so that concrete goes over undisturbed ground. Backfill with 4 inches of granular materials (sand, gravel, crushed stone, or slag) if the surface is not compacted. Use reinforcing mesh to add strength to the slab, even if this isn't required by local building codes.

Specify ready-mix concrete with a minimum bearing capacity of at least 3,500-4,000 psi (pounds per square inch). Driveways used by cars, vans, or pickup trucks should be 4 inches thick; 6 to 8 inches might be necessary to support heavy trucks—ask your contractor. Depending on temperature and humidity, curing time is 5-7 days.

ASPHALT

Asphalt has enough flexibility to conform to slight deviations in the subsurface. Like concrete, hot-mix asphalt can be applied over undisturbed ground that's had vegetation and topsoil stripped away. If the ground is less stable, lay down 2 inches of rock before laying asphalt. In either situation, spray herbicide on the soil before paving to prevent weeds from later forcing their way through the surface.

Apply 4 inches of hot mix over an undisturbed subsurface; use 2 inches of asphalt over a 2-inch gravel base. The pavement may be used immediately after compacting. After one summer passes, seal the surface with a tar-based sealer mixed with sand.

LOOSE FILL

Install curbing—either bricks or pressure-treated wood—on both sides of the driveway to retain the fill. Preparation of the subsurface isn't crucial, although you should level high spots and fill low ones with sand or a mixture of sand and crushed limestone. Saturate the soil with weed killer, then add a 2-inch sand base.

Have the delivery truck dump several piles of loose fill along the length of your driveway. Then spread the fill with a shovel and smooth it with a rake. With a helper or two, level the fill by dragging a 2x4 that stretches from curb to curb the length of the driveway. Finish by rolling or by driving your car across the surface several times to compact the stones.

SPECIAL CONSIDERATIONS	MAINTENANCE	COST
Install *expansion joints* between new concrete and existing paving or buildings. These fibrous strips absorb the loads created when the concrete expands. *Control joints* are necessary to help regulate cracking as the slab settles. Cracks that follow these shallow grooves are easier to repair. Ask your contractor to texture the surface with a *broom finish* for better slip resistance. A soft-bristled broom is used for a light texture; a broom with stiffer or steel bristles creates a heavier texture.	Small cracks are easily repaired with patching cement or latex-cement mix. If the pavement is crumbling or is cracked and settling, the entire damaged section will have to be replaced. Salt and some deicing compounds used in the winter can damage the surface.	In most parts of the country, concrete is the most expensive paving material. Ready-mix concrete is sold by the cubic yard and is delivered to the job site by truck.
Because asphalt is flexible, no expansion joints are needed. In some areas asphalt contractors recommend using 2 inches of hot mix with large aggregate under a 1- to 2-inch finish mix. If you want a colored surface, use an emulsion sealer put on with a squeegee; be prepared for the emulsion to wear off first in high-traffic areas, leaving a patchy-looking surface.	Asphalt should be sealed about every three years, or when the surface turns gray or hairline cracks appear. Use a tar-based sealer mixed with sand; apply with a squeegee when the outdoor temperature is higher than 60° F. Cracks and chuckholes can be filled with asphalt mix sold in bags; rarely do entire sections need to be replaced. Asphalt is impervious to the salt used for deicing.	Asphalt costs less than concrete and is also delivered to the site by truck. Hot-mix asphalt is sold by the ton; 1 ton of material spread 2 inches thick will cover about 100 square feet.
Mineral loose-fill materials are much easier to install than concrete or asphalt. Don't use loose fill on a steeply graded driveway, though—erosion will be a problem.	Rake the fill level every spring and fall; add fill where necessary and compact it with your car.	Sold by the ton, loose fill varies in coverage according to the size of the aggregate. Your supplier will know how much you need if you supply the basic dimensions (length, width, and thickness) of your planned driveway.

CARS AT YOUR HOUSE

OFF-STREET PARKING

If you have more cars than places to keep them in your garage, additional open-air off-street parking is a must. That's particularly true if your community doesn't allow overnight parking on the street or if all cars must be removed from the street when sweepers or snowplows have to get through.

Carefully planned off-street parking might be just the beginning of a whole-yard landscaping project. For example, as you remodel your yard to allow more room for cars, you also can set aside a spot for children's play, include space for a patio where you can relax in comfort, or add trees and shrubs to improve your home's appearance.

The nicely planned area shown *above* illustrates how a two-car, concrete parking zone was combined with a private courtyard in front of the house. Cedar fencing topped with redwood latticework shields the area from public view; an

intercom, buzzer, and light at the gate help the homeowners maintain security.

Living out of town on a larger parcel of land requires different solutions to parking problems from those you'd turn to in more densely settled areas. Obviously, you'll want to have plenty of parking near the house, and you may want to incorporate a circular driveway or a turnaround so guests and delivery trucks don't have to back up long distances when they leave. Also, given the probable length of your driveway, durable, low-maintenance paving materials are particularly important if you want to keep future repair costs down.

The back-to-nature retreat pictured *at left* spreads out to take full advantage of its site. Although the double-width driveway includes extra parking places and a circle in front of the house, the overall landscaping theme absorbs the mass of the asphalt paving. Note, too, that the garage shelters the main entry and doesn't interfere with the family's spectacular view of mountains and surrounding countryside.

THE CARPORT

Although a carport may seem to be little more than a roof over your car, it also can be the starting point for a multipurpose addition to your home. Even if you're not planning any other major projects in the future, you can plan your carport to be a problem-solver. For example:

• Include a large, lockable storage cabinet for bicycles, outdoor cooking tools, lawn and garden equipment, and patio furniture.

• Install gates, or fence in open sides of a carport to create an oversized outdoor playpen for young children.

• Extend the carport roof to cover a backyard patio or play area.

• Use one wall of the carport as the beginning of a screened porch.

• Think about whether you might like to enclose your carport later for garage space or expanded family living room.

The carport pictured *at right*, for example, shelters both the car and the entrance to the patio. The carport's roof reduces summer air-conditioning costs by shading windows along the front of the house.

Although carport architecture is usually very straightforward, it needn't be dull or detract from your home's appearance. For example, the Spanish-style tile-roofed carport shown *above* has all the charm of the main house. Equally important, it ties into both the side of the house and an existing garage, providing the perfect solution for a two-car family with a one-car garage. Last but not least, the homeowners can unload groceries directly into the kitchen.

GARAGE-PLANNING BASICS

Garages are good for cars; they help protect them and make them easier to start in winter. It's for good reason, then, that garages are valued features in virtually all homes. In fact, a properly planned garage could be one of the harder-working areas at your house.

If you don't have a garage, building one may cost less than you'd expect. Because garage-building costs per square foot are much lower than those for standard room additions, you can get a lot of utility for relatively little cost. To get the most for your money, stretch the length and width of your garage to incorporate storage, workshop, and hobby areas that won't fit within your present home. As long as you're building, contemplate building up, adding a loft for a home office, apartment, or "get away from it all" space.

Next, think about the best location for your garage. Make a to-scale site plan that includes your house, driveway, and any plantings you'd like to preserve. If possible, position your garage so it protects the house by blocking winter winds and providing shade from summer sun. Check the path people will follow from the garage to the house, examine the need for a side- or rear-entry door on the garage, and determine the location of windows. Also evaluate your options for exterior siding, trim, and roofing.

Then take your sketch outside, drive four stakes into the ground to mark the structure's four corners, and run string between them for a life-size look at your garage.

Once you have an idea of where your garage should go and how big it will be, sketch a scaled floor plan on graph paper. This plan will come in handy later, when you need to get estimates from a home center or bids from builders or contractors. Use the dimensions on the drawings *at right* as minimum guidelines, and, if you plan to use the garage for more than just cars, consider these factors.

• *Lighting*. Will natural light from a couple of windows be enough, or do you need supplemental fixtures? Four-foot-long fluorescent shop lights provide lots of light at low cost.

• *Wiring*. If you're planning a shop, you'll need outlets for items such as a shop vacuum and power tools, and possibly special wiring for a welder or heavy-duty equipment.

• *Ventilation*. If you want a shop or hobby area that will be used for stripping and refinishing furniture, painting projects, or handling other chemicals, include windows in opposite sides of the garage for cross-ventilation, or install a wall-mounted exhaust fan.

• *Plumbing*. A washtub in a corner of the garage is great for a quick cleanup after you've been working outside. Consider putting a drain in the center of the floor, too, to take care of melting snow that's fallen off your cars.

• *Heating*. If you intend to spend a lot of time in the garage, insulate its walls and ceiling to the minimum standards for your locale, whether you're ducting in warmed air from your home's central heating system or providing a supplemental heater. Insulate and weather-strip the garage door.

Before you call any contractors or price materials, take your plan to the local building inspector's office. You'll need a building permit, and the office may suggest changes that will help your project conform to zoning ordinances, building codes, and neighborhood deed restrictions.

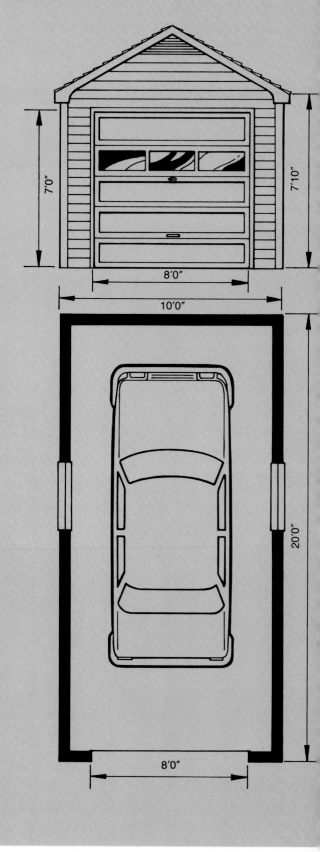

GARAGES: NUMBERS TO KNOW

ONE-CAR GARAGE

TWO-CAR GARAGE

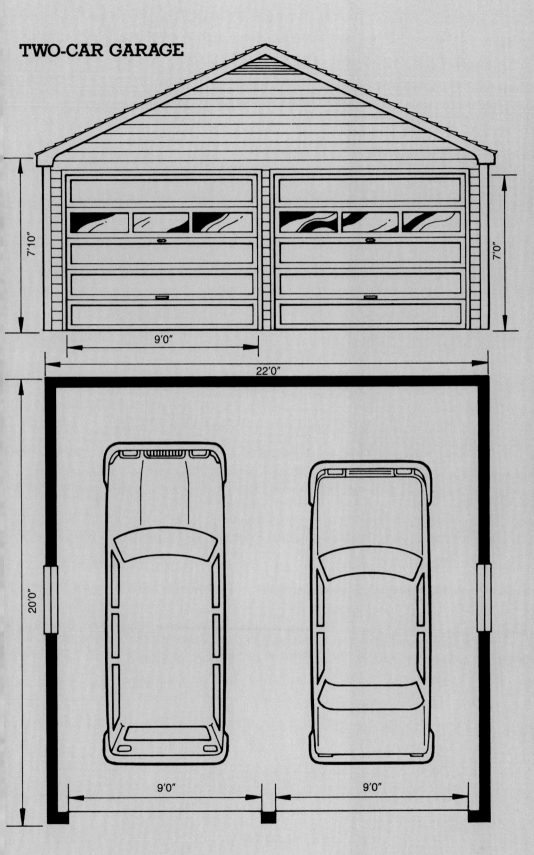

GARAGE DOORS

Garage doors come in a wide variety of materials, including wood, aluminum, steel, fiberglass, molded polyethylene, and other manufactured materials. The two major types are swing-up and roll-up; side-hinged doors are rarely used today. Whatever material and type you choose, installing a garage door is a job best left to professionals.

Ready-made garage doors come in several sizes. The common widths for one-car garage doors are 8, 9, and 10 feet. Double doors generally are 16 or 18 feet wide; you also can use two single doors for a two-car garage, as pictured here.

The standard heights for garage doors are 6½ feet and 7 feet. If you have a taller vehicle, you may want 8-foot-high doors, which are available from some sources.

THE DETACHED GARAGE

When you think about detached garages, you should see more than images of big, tacky boxes devoid of redeeming architectural value. The detached garage pictured *at right*, for example, makes a high-style statement by echoing the shape, roofline, and exterior finish of the house it accompanies. Even the garage door contributes with a surface treatment that matches the privacy fence between the garage and the house.

Although building a garage may seem at first to be too great an undertaking for your construction skills, consider doing all or some of the work yourself. Home centers sell complete garage packages that take the difficulty out of ordering materials, and you can get the job done using common construction techniques.

Working alone or with a couple of helpers, you can complete the work during several evenings or a few weekends. Consider spending the weekend working on an old-fashioned garage raising with a group of volunteers.

If you'd rather leave garage building to experts, select a company that specializes in garages or a contractor.

No matter who builds your garage, the basic procedures are the same.

• *Step 1.* Excavate and pour the concrete footings and slab about a week before building is to begin.

• *Step 2.* Frame the walls and roof; if your budget will stand it, buy prebuilt roof trusses to save hours of measuring, cutting, and fitting.

• *Step 3.* Apply the siding and roofing.

• *Step 4.* Add trim, doors, gutters, and hardware; finish as desired.

CARS AT YOUR HOUSE

THE ATTACHED GARAGE

Although it's usually included as an integral element of a new home, an attached garage also can be added to an existing home as part of a major remodeling. When you're planning your addition, keep in mind that an attached garage can account for a third or more of your home's streetside appearance, which means that the garage's facade must complement the architecture of your house. Consider the impact of the garage door or double doors on the overall design, too. A door that's too ornate can draw attention to itself like a bull's-eye, instead of enhancing exterior styling.

The two-car garage shown *at right* illustrates how planning can pay big dividends when it comes to curb appeal. The garage's exterior repeats the Colonial design theme of the house; locating the double doors away from the street minimizes the mass of the garage and draws attention to the house's front entry. Shrubs further mask the garage.

Preconstruction planning also is especially important to the inside of an attached garage. For example, local building codes may specify a finished fire wall between the garage and the house, fully finished sidewalls and ceiling, or a garage floor that's situated below the home's floor level to keep fumes from seeping into the house.

Analyze traffic flow, too. The entrance from the garage to the house should go directly to the kitchen (or through a mudroom to the kitchen), so you don't have to carry a carload of groceries too far.

SECURITY

Although it's a big consideration for any garage, security is especially important in a structure that's attached to your house. An intruder who isn't brave enough to break a window or pry open a door on your house might find courage inside a garage that allows a door to be jimmied without anyone noticing.

Here are some pointers on burglar-proofing your garage.
• Keep your garage door locked, even when you're at home. Invest in a remote-control garage door opener. You can install it yourself on a Saturday afternoon.
• Hang curtains over garage windows so no one can see when your car is gone. Install break-resistant acrylic plastic on the inside of all windows.
• Keep power tools and other expensive items locked in the house.
• Provide outdoor lighting fixtures that illuminate all door and window areas.
• Buy a tamper-proof alarm system that an intruder can't disconnect without setting it off.

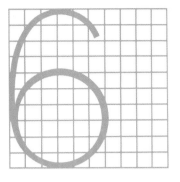

EXTERIOR MAINTENANCE

Maybe it's a spot up under the eaves that defies repainting, a sagging gutter that dribbles water, or a cracked front step. From time to time, most of us notice parts of a home's exterior that need attention, and promise ourselves that we'll get around to dealing with them "one of these days." Instead of making casual observations and equally vague resolves, why not get on top of maintenance chores by methodically examining your home's exterior each spring and fall? Semiannual inspections can help you find problems and solve them before they deteriorate into situations that require costly repairs. This chapter tells how to conduct an inspection, and what to do about what you find.

FIRST, CONDUCT A THOROUGH VISUAL INSPECTION

To make a visual inspection of items that typically call for maintenance, you need only walk slowly around your home and examine each of its elements. With the help of binoculars you probably can do all your checking from the ground. (If you must go up on the roof, wear shoes with non-slip soles, and climb carefully.)

To help organize your search, we've developed a checklist that breaks inspection into zones. The points below correspond to the illustration *opposite*. Use the results of your survey to establish your own maintenance agenda, then refer to the pages that follow for how-to specifics.

Siding and other surfaces. Stains and blemishes can indicate deeper problems, such as moisture seepage. Expect to find some minor cracks in wood siding, but don't worry about them unduly. However, keep in mind that wide cracks or split boards let in water, which can lead to rotting. In masonry, crevices may mean a wall is merely settling slightly, or they could indicate more serious trouble. If you have doubts, consult an expert. More about siding and masonry on pages 82–85.

Exterior paint. All paint deteriorates as it ages, so don't be dismayed by minor imperfections. Other problems, such as mildew, require attention. Peeling paint or a fast-fading finish signals that it's time to repaint. More about paint and paint problems on pages 86 and 87.

The roof. Starting at ridges, look for curled or missing shingles. Check flashings for cracks and holes. Damaged paint at soffits may mean poor attic ventilation or a roof leak draining into the soffit. Ridge-boards and fascia protect shingle edges, so watch for breaks at these locations. Dull shingle surfaces mean extreme wear; reroofing is in order. More about roofing maintenance on pages 88 and 89.

Gutters and downspouts. Sagging or blocked gutters let water leak. Look for loose hangers and disconnected sections. Holes can be mended and sections replaced. For more about gutters and spouts, see pages 90 and 91.

Windows. Dried-out or missing caulk around casings lets air leak in. Check weather stripping and how snugly storm windows fit. Cracked or missing glass must be replaced. Drip caps and sills should be sound. More about windows on pages 92 and 93.

Walks, steps, and drives. Settled steps and pavement are dangerous but can be reset. Frost causes cracks and chuckholes, so plan on patching as necessary. Check to see if a driveway needs resealing. What's the condition of concrete surfaces? More about all of these on pages 94 and 95.

General maintenance. New growth on foundation plantings should be trimmed back. Rails and metalwork may need repainting. If you have central air conditioning, remove obstructions from the condensing unit. Determine whether doors need weather stripping and adjustment. More about miscellaneous outside maintenance jobs on pages 96 and 97.

MAINTAINING SIDING AND MASONRY

Wood, vinyl, or metal siding, shingles, and masonry veneer are more than decorative: They protect your home from water and other weather-related wear and tear. If these coverings are not kept in good condition, your home's structure can be exposed to moisture and rot. That's why preventive maintenance is so important.

The elements of wall construction explained below are pretty much the same whatever the exterior material.

Studs, vertical 2x4s or 2x6s spaced 16 or 24 inches apart, form the framing. Running horizontally beneath the studs is a 2x4 or 2x6 *sole plate*, which is the base of the wall. A *box sill* of larger-dimension lumber and a *sill plate* anchor the wall to the foundation. A *sill seal* keeps moisture outside the foundation.

Above the wall studs is a *top plate*, which carries the load of the rafters or the weight of a second story. Tucked between the studs is *insulation. Sheathing* is fastened to the outside of the studs to add strength and provide more insulation. Asphalt-base *building paper* goes between the sheathing and the exterior siding or masonry.

The enemies list

Kept dry, a wall's structure should last almost indefinitely. However, water, working its way in through the siding or elsewhere, can cause rot and severe damage to wood components, insulation, and even interior surfaces.

Insect damage is another common menace. Termites and carpenter ants are the most common sources of damage. It's important to make annual inspections of your home to check for

signs of their presence and activity. See page 153 for more about these pests and how to deal with them.

Cleaning siding

A sturdy extension ladder and a garden hose with a long-handled car-washing brush are all you need to wash down your home's exterior. Using a mild detergent solution, begin up high and work down, moving the brush in the same direction that the siding runs. Some house paints are self-cleaning, that is, they *chalk* or wear away a little with each rain. Give attention to areas that are unlikely to be washed naturally—eaves, porches, and overhangs. Rinse the siding thoroughly.

If you encounter dark, rash-like stains that won't wash off, suspect *mildew,* a fungus that thrives in areas with high humidity and little sunlight. Masonry surfaces sometimes suffer from another type of blemish called *efflorescence,* a white, powdery lime residue that resists scrubbing. Mildew and efflorescence can be treated as explained in the illustration *at right.*

Other problems you're also likely to encounter as you scrub are noted in the illustration. Put a few tools in a bucket for on-the-spot repairs—include galvanized nails and wood screws, a hammer, a screwdriver, a hand drill (or a cordless electric drill), caulk cartridges and a caulking gun, a wire brush, and a heavy sponge. Note any needed major repairs and leave them for another day. Pages 84 and 85 tell about major repair jobs.

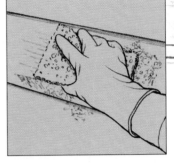

Treating mildew. With household bleach or trisodium phosphate mixed with water, scrub dark spots that resist ordinary washing.

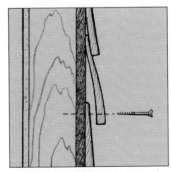

Refastening warped boards. Nails won't hold, so draw the boards back with rustproof screws in predrilled holes. Sink heads, caulk or putty, and paint.

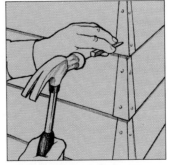

Setting popped nails. Use a hammer and nail set to sink popped nails. Prime and paint nailheads and any bare metal. Caulk and paint cracks and knots.

Cleaning siding. Start at the top and work down with a mild detergent solution. Stroke parallel to the direction of siding, then rinse thoroughly.

Trimming shrubs. To avoid trapping moisture in the foundation and siding, and to reduce wear from rubbing, shear branches clear of the house.

Scouring brick efflorescence. Wearing gloves, brush away powdery areas with a 1-to-10 solution of muriatic acid and water. Clean a small area at a time. Rinse well.

Checking masonry. To see if masonry is settling, put a piece of tape over a crack; it will split or twist in a few days if settling is taking place. Loose mortar joints can be repointed.

REPAIRING SIDING

Wood lap siding, often called clapboard or beveled siding, probably covers more homes than all the other types of siding combined. One reason for its popularity, despite the need for regular and frequent maintenance, is that lap siding isn't difficult to repair or replace.

To repair a split or cracked board, coat both edges of the cracked piece with waterproof glue, let dry until tacky, then force the board together and fasten with galvanized nails or rustproof screws. If evidence of the crack remains, fill it with wood putty or caulking. Large holes caused by a dislodged knot should first be filled with oakum, then caulked and painted.

If a board can't be repaired, you'll need to replace it. Replacing a piece of siding is less difficult than it looks. First find out how it is nailed. Nails on lap siding usually pass through only one board, with the nail in the bottom of a board just clearing the top edge of the board beneath. Sometimes, though, the nails penetrate both boards.

To replace siding, you will need a piece of matching siding, a square, a measuring tape, back- or keyhole saw, pry bar, rustproof nails, shims or wedges, roofing cement, and building paper. If your home is an older one, matching the siding size could pose a problem, since siding was often milled to order and then discontinued. You may have to call several lumber dealers before you find what you need.

Replacing wood and asphalt shingles calls for basically the same techniques used with wood lap siding. See the box *opposite* to learn about repairing other types of siding.

REPLACING LAP SIDING

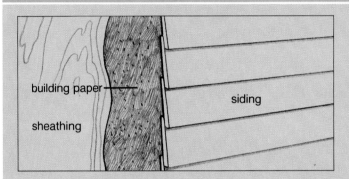

building paper

sheathing

siding

Most exterior walls feature three-layer construction—a stud framework covered by sheathing, a thickness of asphalt-base building paper to keep out moisture, and a final covering of wood siding or other material. Be careful not to damage the building paper during repairs.

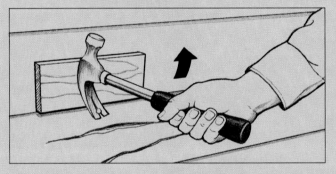

1 Taking out an entire length of siding requires prying up the board above, which holds it in place. Use a pry bar or chisel and go slowly along the board's length to avoid splitting. Protect the siding with a block when pulling nails that come out with the board.

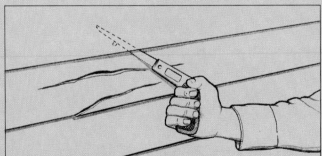

2 Nails that refuse to budge can be cut off by slipping a hacksaw blade underneath. Don't forget to cut the nails on the damaged board, too. Never ruin a good piece of siding by using force to pull stubborn nails.

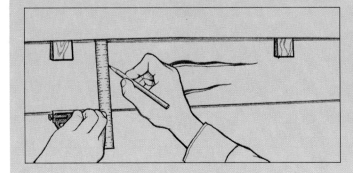

3 If damage occurs only in a portion of the board, tap in wedges under the board above at each edge of the damaged area. Mark saw cuts with a square and use a backsaw to remove the damaged section. Avoid deep cuts that will penetrate the board and building paper beneath.

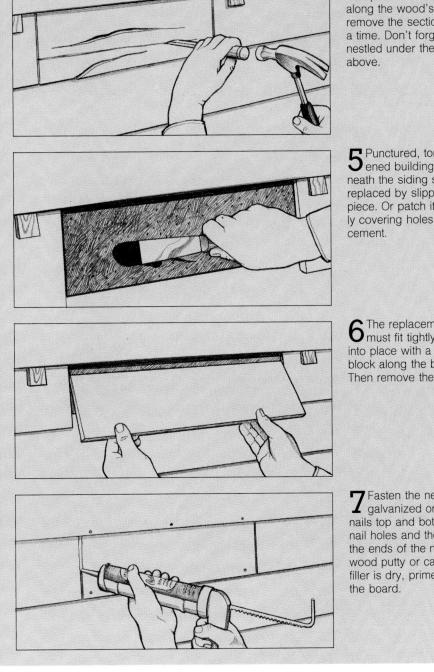

4 With a hammer and chisel, split the damaged area along the wood's grain. Then remove the section a piece at a time. Don't forget the piece nestled under the board above.

5 Punctured, torn, or weakened building paper beneath the siding should be replaced by slipping in a new piece. Or patch it by generously covering holes with roofing cement.

6 The replacement siding must fit tightly. Gently tap it into place with a hammer and block along the bottom edge. Then remove the wedges.

7 Fasten the new board with galvanized or aluminum nails top and bottom, then fill nail holes and the seams at the ends of the new piece with wood putty or caulk. When the filler is dry, prime and paint the board.

REPAIRING MASONRY SURFACES

• *Brick or stone.* To re-point crumbling mortar, clean out loose material in the joint, wet the area, repack it with a mortar mix, then shape the new joints so they match the old ones. For a stronger bond, dampen new mortar at intervals so it takes two or three days to dry.

If long vertical cracks in brick or stonework aren't due to settling, they can be repointed with mortar, but grouting is better, because vinyl-based grout expands and contracts. Before applying grout, remove loose material from the crack with a chisel, and then make a clean sweep with a vacuum. Force the new grout into the crack with a pointing trowel, then smooth the repair.

Chip out old, cracked bricks and replace them, using the method for repointing.

• *Stucco.* Repair small cracks by chipping away loose material, wetting the crack, and applying patching plaster in layers, with ample drying time between applications if the crack is deep. Fix small holes by chipping back to the lath underneath, then building up a new surface in two or three layers with patching cement. Repairing of a few square feet or more is a job for a masonry contractor.

EXTERIOR PAINTING

If your home is in need of a new paint job, you may decide to do the work yourself or hire a contractor. Regardless of who does it, painting a house isn't easy, or inexpensive, but with the high-quality paints available today, you won't have to do the job—or have it done—very often.

Prepping for a paint job

Careful preparation is as important as good-quality materials to the success of any paint job. First, repair damaged siding and set popped nails, as explained on pages 84 and 85. Next, examine the finish itself, which might be suffering any of the problems discussed on the opposite page. Take areas of blemished finish down to bare wood by peeling paint with a putty knife, scraping, sanding, or blistering with an electric paint softener. Keep in mind that the edges of solid paint next to bare wood must be sanded lightly, so new and old surfaces will blend unobtrusively.

Next, give the exterior a good washing with a mixture of trisodium phosphate (TSP) and water to remove dirt and gloss. Remove screens and other detachables so they won't interrupt work flow. Mask or remove lighting fixtures, the mailbox, and house numbers. Use a whisk broom to knock off any dirt missed by washing, and carry the broom with you during painting to dislodge debris missed earlier. Double-check for unprimed areas, bare metal, cracks needing caulking, and other imperfections.

Wait for a dry day, then paint from the upper sections down, trying to remain in the shade. Plan your work so that at day's end you stop on a full course of siding; otherwise you'll have lap marks.

Remove and mask. Mask light fixtures or remove them. Take off screens, storms, mailbox, house numbers, and other things that will slow the painting.

Clean siding. Wash the house from top to bottom with a hose and brush. Remove any clinging debris. Wait a day to paint solvent-based paints.

Remove damaged paint. Peel or scrape off raised paint down to bare wood; spot-prime. Caulk cracks, reset popped nails, and trim or pull away shrubbery.

REMEDIES FOR COMMON PAINT PROBLEMS

PEELING

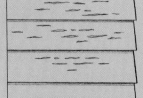

The cause is moisture from within, or finish applied over a wet surface. To prevent a recurrence, install vents in siding, gables, or soffits. Remove the damaged finish to bare wood, prime, and repaint.

ALLIGATORING

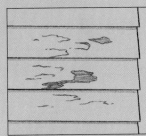

This occurs because the undercoat was not dry or paint was mixed improperly. To remedy, brush or scrape to bare wood, apply primer, and let dry thoroughly.

CHECKING

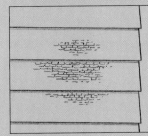

This indicates that siding material has been expanding and contracting. Remove the finish, spot-prime, and let dry. Consider using latex-base house paint, which "gives" with the siding.

BLISTERING

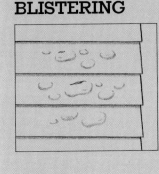

The primer was not completely dry when the finish coat was applied, or the paint was not compatible with its undercoat. Take the finish down to bare wood, prime, and repaint.

BLEEDING

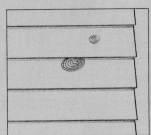

The siding was not cured when installed, and sap is draining from wood, especially knots. Bare the wood, then apply colored shellac or other sealer to the bleeding area before repainting.

NAIL STAINS

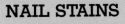

The siding nails are rusting. If stains are localized, pull nails and replace them with aluminum or galvanized nails. Otherwise, sand down the finish to the nailheads, seal with shellac, then repaint.

MILDEW

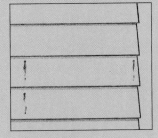

High humidity and moisture from within can cause mildew. Remove stains with bleach and water, let the siding dry, then refinish with mildewcide-treated paint.

CHALKING

Many paints are formulated to clean themselves by eroding. If you are painting over this type of paint, wash the surface thoroughly to remove residue, and let it dry completely before you repaint.

MAINTAINING ROOFS

exhaust

dormer

eav

Roofs take a beating from wind, rain, ice, snow, and—most destructive of all—the sun. But roofs are built to withstand it. A properly laid asphalt or fiberglass shingle roof can last 20 years or more with proper maintenance.

"Out of sight, out of mind" doesn't apply to roof maintenance, because even a small unattended wound in this weatherproof "skin" makes your home's interior vulnerable to moisture. On a shingle roof, the skin is a two-deep, overlapping layer of shingles that covers *roofing felt* laid atop the *sheathing*. Extra shingles cover the *ridge*. Metal or composition *flashings* are tucked under shingles at potential problem areas such as the *valleys,* where two slopes meet, or around chimneys, vents, and other places, where something penetrates the roof. *Fascia* boards offer protection to the shingles at the eaves, and *rake boards* shield the roof's edges. Gutters and downspouts (see pages 90 and 91) channel water away from the roof and to the ground.

Tracing leaks

Water entering through the roof often appears at places some distance from the actual leak. Because water follows a wandering course, check for the leak higher up on the roof than signs indicate. It may show up as a pencil point of light from the attic or crawl space. Or the spot may be damp. Mark a hole by pushing a wire up through it; mark a damp spot by driving a nail through the sheathing and the roof above. Fix leaks by sealing with roof cement or replacing shingles as shown *opposite.*

If your attic is finished or the roof is otherwise closed to inside inspection, wait for a mild,

dry day to get on the roof in search of the leak.

Examining your roof

Twice a year, in spring and fall, give your roof the once-over. If you're not fond of high places, stand on the ground and use binoculars, focusing on the sunny slopes first.

Among the places most likely to need repair are the ridges, where shingles crack and break in the wind. Water entering there can go anywhere.

There are other high-risk areas, too. Valleys often collect leaves and twigs that act as dams; flashings or shingles here can rust through or work loose. Flashings around vents and chimneys should be watertight, rust-free, and sealed with roof cement or caulking compound. Missing, curled, or broken shingles allow water to seep underneath and rot sheathing. Clogged downspouts may force water up and under shingles at a roof's edge. An accumulation of shingle-coating granules in gutters may signal that you'll soon need a new roof.

Making roof repairs

Lifted or split shingles can be relaid with roof cement, a trowel, roofing nails, and a hammer. Pliable shingles are easier to work with, so wait until a warm day, or use a propane torch with a spreader tip to heat shingles. Trowel on cement, nail the shingle into place, then coat the nailheads.

Cover loose edges and small holes in flashings with roof cement. Patch larger holes with flashing material laid in a bed of roof cement. Closed valley flashings require removing shingles to get at the problem.

chimney flashing

vent stack

ridge

rake board

sidewall flashing

Remove damage. To remove a damaged shingle, loosen nails under the shingle above by inserting a spade. Pull the nails and slip out the damaged shingle.

Replace shingle. Measure the area to be covered and cut a piece of shingle to fit tightly. Slip the new shingle in place under the old, aligning it with adjoining shingles.

Cement into place. Nail the shingle down and coat nail-heads with roof cement. Press the top shingle into place; to keep it flat, use a weight until the cement has set.

MAINTAINING GUTTERS

Gutters and downspouts are your roof's drainage system. Exterior and foundation walls, topsoil, and plantings would all be periodically drenched if water simply cascaded off the roof. Familiarize yourself with a gutter system's components, as illustrated *opposite,* then consider these maintenance pointers.

• In late fall and again in late spring, inspect gutters and downspouts for leaves, twigs, holes, and sags.

• Sagging gutters leak, so check that all hangers are firmly anchored and attached to the gutter sections. A gutter should slant to its downspout about ⅛ inch for every foot of length. Long runs may be raised in the middle and slant toward a downspout at each end. Wherever a gutter sags, water could collect and rust it through. Correct a sag by bending the gutter's hanger or adding a new hanger.

• Seams where sections join also may leak. Try pushing them back together and re-crimping. Patch a rusted-out gutter on the inside by applying a piece of lightweight metal or roofing paper. Fasten it with bonding adhesive, then seal the patch with more adhesive.

If maintenance comes too late, you will have to replace your gutters and downspouts; your choices are outlined in the chart *below.*

Clean gutters. Remove mud, leaves, and other debris from gutters each spring and fall. Hose gutters clean from the high end of each run. Check for drips.

Clear downspouts. Blockage in a downspout can be blasted free with hose pressure. If a jam is stubborn, you may have to use a plumber's snake to break it up.

COMPARING GUTTER MATERIALS

	FEATURES	MAINTENANCE	LIFE SPAN/COST
STEEL	Either baked-on enamel or galvanized finishes.	Requires periodic painting to prevent rust.	15 years or so; inexpensive option.
ALUMINUM	Not as strong as steel, but popular. Enamel or plastic-clad finishes. Easy to handle.	Corrosion-resistant but may need repainting.	15-20 years; moderately priced.
VINYL	Tricky to install, but durable. Few colors.	Impervious to elements. Won't accept paint.	Available with lifetime warranty. Expensive.
COPPER	Durable but not popular. Joints soldered.	No corrosion, but joints need resoldering.	At least 50 years. Very expensive.
WOOD	Heavy. Compatible with appearance of old houses.	Requires annual attention. Warping is common.	10-15 years. Moderate.

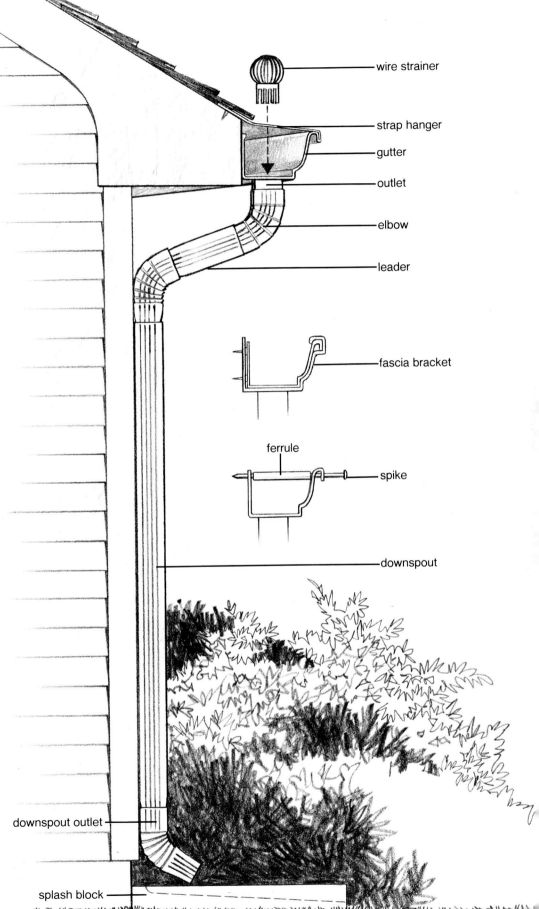

wire strainer

strap hanger

gutter

outlet

elbow

leader

fascia bracket

ferrule

spike

downspout

downspout outlet

splash block

Seal leaks. Scrape and wire-brush rusted areas in gutters. A thin coat of roofing cement will protect and seal the metal.

Install leaf screens. Leaf screens keep gutters flowing freely. Slip them under shingles and fasten with roofing nails. Seal the nailheads.

Adjust splash guards. Raise splash blocks, shown *above* and *at right,* to keep water away from the foundation. Shim the block, then fill underneath with gravel or sand.

MAINTAINING WINDOWS

Besides giving you a view of the outside world, windows let in light and refreshing breezes, and keep out the elements. Through both heat loss and air leaks (see the illustration *below*), windows also influence how much heat your home retains.

Heat loss occurs through the glass windowpanes. One of the best ways to retard this is to add more layers of glazing that trap air between them.

Short of replacing single-thickness glass with double-or triple-thickness insulating glass, the only way to add more glazing to existing windows is to install storm windows.

In summer, single-thickness glass gains heat. An older home with air conditioning and this type of glass will benefit by having storms on all year.

Seal air leaks around window frames and sashes with weather stripping and caulking. Weather stripping, applied at window jambs, where sashes meet, and on the sill, comes in spring metal and "gasket" types. Both types are easy but time-consuming to install. Spring metal weather stripping lasts longer and is less obtrusive.

Another way to cut air leaks is to replace any loose glazing compound around windowpanes. Recaulk around and under exterior window casings and sills as necessary.

Check removable storm windows seasonally for fit and the condition of their glazing and paint. If you have combination storms and screens, you'll need to check mechanisms, fastenings, and glazing annually. The caulking around metal frames where combinations are attached to the window casing often dries out and requires renewing.

Before the heat of summer, you'll also want to check screens for holes and tears, and mend or replace screening as needed. Steel screens should be repainted as necessary with a screen paint and an applicator pad.

PLUGGING AIR LEAKS

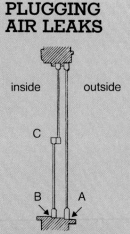

inside   outside

Exterior storm windows are your first line of defense against heat loss. Trap insulating air between interior and exterior glazing by concentrating your weatherstripping efforts at the points shown in the drawing *above*.
A. Install weather stripping at the bottom of the lower sash.
B. A tight fit at the sill prevents air from leaking through the window.
C. A snug latch and weather stripping seals the gap where sashes meet.

COMMON SEALANTS

	WHERE TO USE	COST
OIL-BASE	Once favored because it bonds to most surfaces, but there are now superior products, such as the ones discussed below.	Inexpensive.
ACRYLIC LATEX	Paintable, fast-drying, all-purpose sealant for cracks and joints that are not constantly exposed to water.	Moderately expensive.
VINYL LATEX	Water- and weatherproof, with high adhesion. Excellent for sealing around exterior window frames.	Moderately expensive.
BUTYL	Adheres to unlike surfaces, such as wood and metal. Use around flashings, storm windows. Flexible and paintable.	Moderately expensive.
SILICONE	Long-lasting elasticity and great adhesion. Waterproof. Usually unpaintable.	Very expensive.

ANATOMY OF A WINDOW

drip cap   head casing   brick molding

head jamb

parting stop

blind stop

sill

inside stop

side casing

side jamb

pane

muntin

sash lock

upper sash

blind stop

lower sash

glazing
compound

parting stop

stool

sill

The drawing *at left* and the detail *above* identify the exterior elements of a window that may require periodic attention.

Start your survey up top. Here you may find a *drip cap,* metal flashing that tucks up under the course of siding just above the window and deflects water from the top edge of its *head casing.* If a drip cap has been damaged or rusted through, water could seep under the casing. (Windows with deep roof overhangs often don't have drip caps.)

Next, check the joint where the *side casings* and your home's exterior covering meet. If caulking here has deteriorated, recaulk.

Now look at the *upper* and *lower sashes.* Are paint and *glazing compound* intact? If not, apply fresh compound and repaint.

If the upper sash rattles, check the *parting stop* that guides its inner side and the *blind stop* outside. Loose stops should be renailed. (With many windows, the blind stop is an integral part of the casing.)

Finally, take a look at the *sill.* Is paint sound? Has rot set in? Rotted sills can be replaced, capped with metal, or rebuilt with fiberglass patching material. Recaulk under the sill, too, if needed.

MAINTAINING WALKS, STEPS, AND DRIVES

Sealing small cracks. Partially fill small cracks in asphalt with sand; top with the type of liquid sealer that's available in tubes. If there are many tiny cracks, you may have to seal the entire surface.

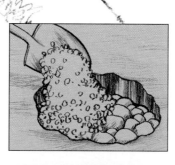

Filling chuckholes. Fill deep chuckholes with rocks and stones; then add gravel to within 4 inches of the surface. Add asphalt mix in layers, tamping in between, until the patch mounds above the surface.

Sealing wider cracks. Use a paste of sand and sealer to fill cracks wider than ⅛ inch. With a trowel, pack the mixture into the crack and tamp to compact.

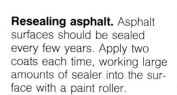

Smoothing patch. First sprinkle the fresh asphalt with sand to limit tracking. Drive your car back and forth over the surface to compact the patch.

Resealing asphalt. Asphalt surfaces should be sealed every few years. Apply two coats each time, working large amounts of sealer into the surface with a paint roller.

Few materials around your home are as tough and durable as those used for walks, steps, and drives. Concrete, asphalt, stone, and brick stand up well to use and abuse. Most of the damage they do suffer is caused by the power of frost, which can heave and split rigid surfaces in contact with the ground. Left unattended, even small fissures in asphalt can turn into chuckholes. Cracks in concrete collect water, freeze, and widen.

Despite its susceptibility to chuckholes, asphalt is flexible enough to ride out major frost damage. When cracks and holes do appear they should be repaired as soon as temperatures rise above 70 degrees, the temperature at which asphalt becomes workable. Fill cracks as shown in the two illustrations *opposite, far left*.

Chuckholes must be dug out to solid material before being repaired. If they are deep, first fill the bottom with stones to save material, then add gravel to within four inches of the surface. Pour premixed asphalt compound in the hole, slicing it from time to time with a spade or trowel to dispel air pockets. Tamp to pack the mix as you go, stopping an inch from the

top. Mound the final layer above the surface, then tamp firmly. Spread sand over the completed patch and pack it further with your car.

Resealing asphalt paving every few years keeps it flexible and extends its life. Buy large buckets of the preparation and coat the surface as shown *opposite*.

Once concrete steps and sections of walkways settle or heave, they become dangerous; left unattended they can deteriorate to the point that they have to be replaced. Before realigning steps or slabs, as shown *at right*, determine why they have moved. Sections of fill underneath the concrete may have washed out or shifted. Tree roots may be pushing up from below. Add fill or remove the roots before you attempt repairs.

Stains, although not safety- or structure-threatening, are unsightly, and concrete walks, steps, and patios seem to collect them. Most stains can be removed with dishwashing detergent and water applied with a stiff brush. You may need to use ammonia or mineral spirits to get rid of stubborn stains. As a last resort, use a 1-to-1 solution of muriatic acid and water; wear rubber gloves while you work.

Patching concrete. To repair concrete, you first have to cut back the damaged area to solid material. Before patching crumbled spots, chip off loose pieces, then trowel on a mixture of epoxy cement and sand. Feather the edges.

Releveling steps. Lift up settled steps with a crowbar, then shim or fill underneath with stones or sand. Fill the joints between steps and a foundation with caulk to stop moisture from seeping in and causing damage.

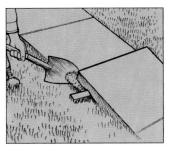

Repairing walkways. To repair sunken walkway sections, lift, prop, and rebuild the bed with a dry mix of sand, earth, and cement. Overfill to allow for settling.

MAINTAINING: TOP TO BOTTOM

When you're planning your maintenance schedule, it's a good idea to start at the top. Check chimneys, vents, stacks, and other roof penetrations for obstructions several times a year. Install caps and protective screens to keep pests out and gases freely flowing. Also keep in mind that regular use of a fireplace can clog screens in chimney caps with soot and ash, making seasonal cleaning a necessity.

Once you're on the roof, make a full inspection. Look at all flashings, especially around the chimney. If you doubt their ability to keep out water, coat them with roof cement. If you see crumbling mortar between chimney bricks, repoint as soon as possible. Secure attachments such as television antennas; retighten or replace fittings and to be sure to test any guy wires.

Peeling paint on soffits is a sure sign of inadequate attic ventilation or water leaking in through the roof. Clear any blockages from existing vents; if vents are bent or damaged, replace them. Plan to install additional venting if your attic has less than one square foot of vent for each 300 feet of attic floor space. If there's no vapor barrier between the roof and attic air space, you'll need double that amount of venting. Ask a dealer about the types of vents available.

Down to earth

After you've worked your way back to ground level, check the weather stripping on windows and doors. Don't neglect rear entry doors and those that lead to the garage or basement.

Existing weather stripping, commonly of spring metal, can be bent back into shape by gentle prying with a screwdriver. If it's missing or beyond repair, attach new material. Look over the various types at your lumber or hardware dealer. Some of the best insulators, such as "J-strips," are the most difficult to install. Foam tape is easiest to apply but has a limited life span. A variety of special devices is available for sealing the bottoms of doors.

Door hardware requires occasional maintenance also. Adjust and tighten hinges, and check the alignment of locks and stops. Lubricate closers on storm/screen doors each spring and fall, as shown *opposite, lower near right*. If closer hardware has pulled loose, refasten it.

Metalwork

Metal railings, patio furniture, downspouts, and other fixtures weather and need attention. Paint will brighten old finishes, but it won't last long unless you do the job properly. Because metals oxidize, most paints won't adhere well unless the metal has been properly primed. Strip severely rusted iron or steel before you start painting, and be sure to use an appropriate metal primer before applying a finish coat. Some surfaces, such as aluminum, require buffing with steel wool. A coat of clear auto polish keeps aluminum shiny. Copper or brass can be painted with polyurethane after cleaning.

Clean around air conditioning condenser. Before each cooling season, cut back shrubs, vines, and long grasses around the outside condensing unit of central air conditioning systems. Remove leaves and other debris from vents for full airflow and efficiency. Check the slab for settling.

Check soffit vents. Clear and repair soffit vents, or replace them if they are severely damaged. Peeling paint could indicate inadequate attic ventilation. Install more or larger vents before repainting.

Protect metal surfaces. Clean iron or steel surfaces with a wire brush before refinishing. Prime metal with zinc chromate to ensure a lasting paint job.

Lubricate door closers. Closers on combination doors need periodic lubrication. Wipe the shaft with a light machine oil. Adjust the closing mechanism to be sure the door shuts tightly.

Adjust weather stripping. Fit weather stripping at the top and sides of doors as needed. Revive old metal weather stripping by prying it apart as shown. Check the threshold for air leaks and examine caulking around the outside frame.

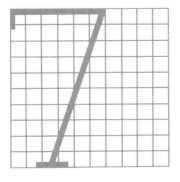

SELECTING & INSTALLING CLADDINGS

Roofing and siding serve as a home's skin, protecting its frame and interior from moisture, cold, and heat. Besides being a home's first line of defense against the elements, claddings also define its appearance. Proper maintenance, as described in the previous chapter, can prolong the life of any cladding, but eventually just about all roofing and siding deteriorate and must be replaced. This chapter surveys your materials options and guides you through the process of installing them.

ROOFING AND SIDING: GENERAL CONSIDERATIONS

Re-covering the outside of your house is one of the most dramatic and possibly one of the most expensive projects you'll face as a homeowner. Deciding which cladding material to invest in demands that you consider appearance, durability, economy, maintenance, and, if you plan to do the job yourself, ease of installation.

First, what's presently covering your house? If the roofing or siding is worn but still provides a smooth, level nailing surface, you may be able to install new materials over the old ones. Some materials can be nailed directly into the old surface. More often, you'll need to put up furring strips, then attach the new cladding to the furring. A double layer of materials increases energy efficiency somewhat; installing extra insulation between the layers can boost it dramatically.

Most homes can withstand the weight of one and possibly two reroofings over the original roof. Beyond that, you'll usually need to remove at least the top layer before installing new materials. Tile and slate roofs are extremely heavy. If your home is not already roofed with one of these materials, its structure probably cannot handle the additional weight without extensive modifications.

With siding, you'll need to compare the time saved by not removing the old cladding with the added time for building out window and door openings to compensate for increased thickness of the walls. Heavy siding materials such as brick or stone veneer require sturdy foundations to support them. If your home never had masonry veneer, you usually can't re-side with it.

One thing you'll want to avoid is merely covering up problems rather than first solving them. If, for example, an old roof has leaked persistently, you'll need to find the source of the leak and repair any damage to insulation, sheathing, and rafters before installing new materials. Otherwise you risk trapping damaging moisture under the new roof. The same can be said for siding.

The layered look

Like a bird's feathers or a fish's scales, siding and roofing rely on layering to keep water from penetrating. Considering the expanse of any home's walls and roof, it would be nearly impossible to cover them in one seamless coating of water-impervious material. Layering lets water run from one board, tile, or shingle to another until it reaches the ground. Overlapping horizontal courses and staggering vertical seams minimizes water infiltration. Even where the exterior surface is smooth, as it is with hardboard or plywood panel siding, you'll find layering underneath in the form of overlapping sheets of building paper.

Choosing materials

You can select natural materials, or choose manufactured products that simulate the appearance of wood, slate, or stucco. The owners of the New England-style home shown *opposite* wrapped it in a variety of materials. Up top, asphalt roofing replicates the look of cedar shingles. Cedar siding, stained green, covers the garage in the foreground. On the wing at the rear of the photograph, hardboard siding imitates clapboard.

The charts on the following pages will help you evaluate a selection of readily available roofing and siding materials.

HOW TO CHOOSE ROOFING AND SIDING MATERIALS

CHOOSING ROOFING MATERIALS

MATERIAL	FEATURES	MAINTENANCE	LIFE SPAN/COST
ASPHALT, ASPHALT/ FIBERGLASS SHINGLES	Traditional asphalt shingles are made of organic (wood-fiber base) roofing felt, saturated with asphalt and surfaced with ceramic-coated mineral granules. These granules give the shingles their characteristic surface appearance and a wide range of variegated colors.	Asphalt shingles require little maintenance at first; eventually some shingles may crack, warp, curl, or begin to lose surface granules. Repairs are fairly easy and usually involve re-nailing or replacing worn shingles. (See pages 88 and 89 for details.)	Asphalt shingles can last from 15-30 years. Top-of-the-line fiberglass-base shingles have the longest life span. With organic-base shingles, better quality ones are heavier.
WOOD SHINGLES AND SHAKES	Usually made of cedar, a lightweight wood with natural preservatives that resist decay. Shingles are sawed on both surfaces and present a smooth, uniform appearance. Shakes feature at least one split surface and give a rugged, hand-hewn look.	Clean the roof annually; moist debris such as leaves or needles can cause deterioration or stain-ing. Most cedar roofs are left un-treated, but fungicides should be applied at least every five years in hot, humid regions where mildew is a problem.	If well maintained, shin-gles can last 20 years or more; shakes, up to 50 years. Cedar's strength and rigidity help it resist damage from wind or hail. Cost is moderate to expensive.
SLATES AND CLAY TILES	Kiln-fired ceramic clay tiles come in half-cylinders or flat shingles. Quarried roofing slates are cut into flat squares or rectangles. Slates and tiles are now available with prepunched nail holes.	Tiles and slates are brittle, so a few may crack or chip over the lifetime of the roof. Repairs are tricky and best left to profession-als. Avoid walking on these roofs; the surface is fragile and slippery.	If you make repairs immediately, before the underlayment is dam-aged, slate and tile roofs can last the lifetime of your house.
METAL	Most metal roofs installed today are aluminum, but you also can use stainless steel, copper, galvanized steel, or steel coated with terne, an alloy of lead and tin. Overlapping ribbed panels, metal shakes, or shingles also are available.	Wind-blown objects can some-times cause dents or damage. Repairs are not difficult. Depend-ing on the type of roof, they involve simply replacing panels, or patching with soldered metal or fiberglass.	Aluminum roofs can last up to 35 years; copper and alloys, even longer. Cost is moderate to expensive depending on the metal selected.
ROLL AND BUILT-UP ROOFING	Roll roofing is similar in composition to traditional asphalt shingles, but comes in wide strips that are over-lapped horizontally to cover the roof surface. It has a drab, utilitarian ap-pearance best suited for roofs with very shallow slopes. Used only on flat or slightly sloped surfaces, built-up roofing consists of layers of or-ganic- or fiberglass-base felt laminated with asphalt or coal tar, usually topped with gravel.	Cracks, tears, and blisters develop, especially in lightweight, single-layer installations. Repairs involve patching with roof cement and new roofing materials. With built-up roofs, leaks can develop from poor application and, be-cause of the gravel topcoat, may be difficult to trace. Repairs are similar to those used for roll roofing.	Roll roofing can last from 5 to 15 years depending on quality. Check whether the com-pany that installs the roofing includes patch-ing with warranties. Built-up roofing lasts from 5 to 20 years. In general, the more layers, the longer the roof's life expectancy.

CHOOSING SIDING MATERIALS

MATERIAL	APPEARANCE	FEATURES	LIFE SPAN/COST
LUMBER	Solid lumber siding is the aristocrat of wood claddings. Species include redwood, cedar, cypress, pine, fir, spruce, hemlock, and more. Redwood, cedar, and cypress often are left to weather; stain or paint other species.	Lumber siding offers design versatility; many styles can be applied horizontally, vertically, or diagonally. A smooth undersurface is essential; applying over existing siding is difficult. Avoid splitting boards when nailing.	Lumber siding can last the lifetime of your house. Prices range from inexpensive to expensive, depending on the wood species.
PLYWOOD	Made of thin sheets of real wood bonded together with waterproof adhesive, plywood siding comes in 4x8-, 4x9-, or 4x10-foot panels. Plywood panels offer as many species varieties as lumber siding.	Large panels speed installation, and result in a minimum of joints; fewer joints reduce air and noise infiltration. Panels can flatten out small imperfections in the undersurface. Plywood can be painted, stained, or left to weather.	May require refinishing, but can last the lifetime of your house. The substrate usually is warranted for 20 years; the finish, 2–5 years.
HARDBOARD	Hardboard is manufactured by compressing wood fibers at high temperatures into sheet goods. Available in lap boards or vertical panels, hardboard features a uniform embossed surface.	Because it is knot- and grain-free, hardboard won't split when nailed. Factory-finished hardboard requires no surface treatment after installation.	Vinyl-clad hardboard carries guarantees up to 30 years. Other types guarantee the substrate for 25 years; the finish coat, for 5–15 years.
WOOD SHINGLES AND SHAKES	Made of cedar, shingles have a smooth, uniform surface; shakes are split, rather than sawed, and have a deeply textured face. Shingles and shakes are typically purchased unfinished, though some have factory-applied colors.	Cedar is naturally resistant to moisture and insect infestation and provides excellent insulation. Shingles and shakes come in various thicknesses and widths, and lengths of 16, 18, and 24 inches.	Shingles and shakes can last the lifetime of your house. Apply mildewcide in humid regions. Moderate to expensive, depending on grade.
METAL	Usually made of aluminum, but sometimes steel, metal siding comes in laps or panels that lock together, and also in shingles in a variety of colors.	Available with baked enamel or vinyl finish. Fireproof and impervious to insects. If not insulated, may be noisy in wind, rain, or hail.	Warranties start at 25 years; some steel and vinyl-clad aluminum sidings come with lifetime guarantees.
VINYL	Available in horizontal lap styles that imitate clapboard, or in vertical styles. Vinyl siding comes in a limited assortment of factory-applied colors, and textures that simulate wood graining.	Color runs throughout the siding so scratches are virtually invisible. Vinyl does not dent the way metal siding can, and does not conduct electricity.	Guaranteed for up to 50 years. Because it expands and contracts more than other materials, correct installation is crucial.

INSTALLING
A NEW ROOF

A sound roof can protect a home for as long as a century. Inspect your roof periodically as described on pages 80 and 88. Minor repairs can stave off replacing a roof for a while, but because roofing tends to wear evenly, serious warnings in some areas often foreshadow deterioration of the entire roof.

Roofing materials are measured in *squares*—a square being the amount of material needed to cover a 100-square-foot area. Taken into account in this figure is the maximum *exposure* recommended by the manufacturer—the distance between the bottom edge of one course of shingles and the bottom edge of the overlapping course.

Manufacturers also often specify the degree of roof slope necessary for a successful installation. Shingles or shakes, for example, can't be used on flat or very shallow roofs because water can back up under the shingles. Entirely flat roofs require built-up roofing or soldered metal; shallow slopes can be covered with asphalt roll roofing. Steeper roofs take almost any material.

Roofing materials are tested by the Underwriters Laboratories (UL) for fire and wind resistance. Class C roofing has passed tests for light fire exposure; Classes B and A will protect against more severe fires. Most residential building codes require roofing rated at least Class C. Shingles that have earned a "wind-resistant" label from UL can withstand test winds of at least 60 miles per hour for two hours without a tab lifting. In warm, humid regions, consider using shingles that have been treated to resist fungus and algae.

Following is a detailed look at how asphalt shingles are installed.

102

1 This asphalt roof has seen better days. Shingles have curled, become brittle, and even broken. They are rapidly losing their protective granule coating. If yours is an aging wood shingle or shake roof, look for dried-out, warped, and broken shingles. Note that the chimney flashing here also is deteriorated. Often flashings also should be replaced at the time a new roof is installed.

2 If your home has asphalt or wood shingles and hasn't been reroofed more than twice, new materials probably can be applied directly over the old; however, even a single layer of shakes must be removed before you can reroof. Regardless of its material, however, a roof must basically be sound and smooth before a new covering is installed. Workmen first remove or nail down any protruding nails.

3 If you're planning to reroof over old shingles, any missing or badly damaged shingles should be replaced, as explained on pages 88 and 89. Old hip and ridge shingles must be removed, too. If drip edges are badly deteriorated, they should be replaced at this time.

4 Usually, new asphalt or wood shingles can be nailed directly to old ones, without a layer of underlayment between them. However, some codes require that you use a No. 30 felt underlayment when reroofing over wood shingles.

5 If your home has shakes or more than three layers of shingles on its roof, your contractor will need to tear off old materials to the sheathing before installing new roofing. That's what happened here. Note that new underlayment also is being installed. Once everything has been removed, workers can check the sheathing and correct any sagging, rot, or water-damage problems.

6 A new roof begins with *starter strips* at the eaves. These are created by removing tabs from ordinary shingles. The strips are bent, then nailed to the edge of the roof, as shown here. The first course of shingles fully overlaps this strip; each succeeding course partially overlaps the one below.

(continued)

INSTALLING
A NEW ROOF
(continued)

7 At vent flashings, roofers first carefully trim shingles to fit, then check their alignment against horizontal and vertical chalk lines. Note the dark lines on these new shingles; they're strips of adhesive that, once melted by the sun, secure the shingles against high winds.

8 Now workers apply asphalt cement around the vent stack, slip a shingle into the cement, press it firmly into place, and then apply more cement. If old stacks are in poor condition, they should be replaced and firmly sealed to the existing surface before new roofing is installed.

9 Valleys, where two roofs intersect, require particular care. Valley treatments differ. Some, like the one shown here, are called "open valleys." With this treatment, shingles overlap flashings made of metal or other materials that bear the brunt of water runoff. "Closed valleys" also include flashings, but, because the shingles from each roof plane butt into each other, you can't see the flashings. With "woven valleys," shingles from each roof plane are interlaced with each other.

10 At ridges, you need a double course of shingles. The first is the one that overlaps the course below it. The second straddles the ridge. Here it's important to keep shingles absolutely straight. First, chalk lines are snapped on either side of the ridge. Next, the roofer cuts shingles to size and bends them in half lengthwise.

11 Ridge shingles should be started at the end opposite prevailing winds. Where hips intersect with a ridge, shingles should be cemented for a watertight seal. Flashing isn't a good idea here because corrosion could discolor the roof.

12 After a roof is completed, it should be swept clean and any debris removed from gutters and valleys. Before the contractor departs, ask for your warranty and a small pile of leftover shingles for any repairs you might need to make later on. Store these in a dry, well-ventilated place. Both asphalt and wood shingles deteriorate in damp or excessively hot environments.

INSTALLING
NEW SIDING

A crew of novice do-it-yourselfers, supervised by a competent woodworker, re-sided the house pictured *above* in two weekends with manufactured hardboard siding that simulates the appearance of weathered cedar. Although the finished installation looks like shingles, the siding actually is lapped boards that come in 8- and 16-foot lengths; embossing creates the rough-textured look of cedar. The siding features a rabbeted top edge, which simplifies installation by making the laps self-aligning, and forms a tight fit at the laps.

To figure out how much siding to buy, the crew determined the total surface area of the house. (To figure how

much surface area the siding must cover, use the formula found on page 50.) Professional contractors deduct a portion of the window and door areas, but novices are better off allowing extra material for mistakes. Order nails at the same time. Use only rustproof nails or staples. Select hot-dipped zinc-coated galvanized types, or nails or staples made of aluminum or stainless steel. Metal fasteners galvanized by electrolysis are not recommended for exterior use.

The homeowner provided power tools, including a circular saw and a saber saw to cut

the siding to fit. Hammers, sawhorses, ladders, and ladder jacks were the only other equipment required.

Storing and handling siding
You'll need to take special precautions to store siding materials of any type. Although wood or hardboard siding braves the elements once it's on your house, it's vulnerable to warping and water and mildew damage prior to installation. Store siding in a dry garage or basement. If indoor storage is not feasible, support the siding off the ground on concrete blocks and securely cover it with heavy plastic sheeting. Aluminum siding can be dented or scratched by

careless handling; vinyl siding can become brittle if exposed to freezing weather.

This home's original siding was of poor quality and badly deteriorated, so it was removed and small tears in the building paper were patched. The photos opposite and on pages 108-109 take you step-by-step through the crew's installation. Procedures vary somewhat from one siding material to another, but generally, most lapped siding goes up this way.

1 Whether you plan to remove the old siding (as was done in this case) or install new cladding over old, you'll need to remove downspouts, decorative trim, shutters, and any other items that interfere with re-siding. If you plan to reuse moldings and trim, remove them very carefully with a pry bar.

With these preparations out of the way, our crew started re-siding by installing corner boards. They used rough-sawn cedar 1x4s, cut to fit. Position the first corner board by holding a level vertically against it. When the board is properly plumbed, nail it securely in place. Next, butt-join the second corner board against the first one, and nail it to the house.

Leave a ⅛-inch gap between the top of the corner boards and the soffit. You'll caulk this expansion gap at the end of the installation.

As an alternative to corner boards, you might choose to cap the corners with metal flashing after the siding is installed, then paint the metal to match.

2 If the builder's original chalk line is still visible and level (as it was on this house), use it as a guide for aligning the first course of siding. If the old chalk line has faded, or isn't straight, you'll have to snap a new one, and check it for level. Before installing the first course of siding, you'll need to nail up a starter strip to angle the bottom of the siding outward. Here, pieces ripped from the old siding were used. The bottom course of siding should overlap the starter strip by about ⅛ inch.

With some siding materials you don't need a starter strip. These should overlap the top of the foundation by 1 inch.

3 It takes several people to maneuver each long piece of siding into position. For the first course, the person at one end nails the siding into place at the bottom edge. Working from end to end, continue nailing the bottom of this course through the starter strip into the studs at 16-inch intervals. With subsequent courses, nails go through the bottom of the upper layer of siding into the rabbeted top edge of the course below it.

If you can't round up a crew to help you with the installation, don't attempt to put up lap siding yourself; the lengths are too unwieldy for a single worker. Choose individual shingles or shakes instead.

(continued)

107

INSTALLING
NEW SIDING
(continued)

4 Vertical joints should always fall over studs; the nailing pattern on the sheathing indicates where studs are located. At vertical joints, you can nail at both the top and bottom of the siding strip if you wish. Butt the next length of siding lightly against the first one—to allow for expansion—and nail it in place.

Vertical joints should be staggered from one course to the next. If vertical joints align, the gaps provide a conduit for water that could then work its way through the siding.

Along the siding's run, between joints, drive nails into each stud. Siding up to 10 inches wide requires two nails per stud; wider versions will need three.

5 Periodically, check courses to be sure they're truly horizontal, especially if your siding's top edges don't automatically ensure equal overlap. If you fail to check for level, you may wind up with a top course that's seriously out of alignment. Then you will have to remove course after course until you find the misaligned one and correct it.

Find true horizontal with a level, then snap a chalk line. If you don't have interlocking siding and want to predetermine exactly where each course will lap, use a story pole—a 1x2 as tall as the height of the wall, on which you've marked the laps. Tack the pole to each corner of the house, copy markings onto the corner boards, and snap chalk lines.

6 If you have an old piece of siding, you can use it as a template to cut pieces to fit the gable and roof peak. You can also use a sliding T-bevel to determine the correct angle and transfer it to the siding, or make templates from heavy brown paper.

To prevent splintering on the "good" side, cut prefinished siding with the finished side down when using a circular saw. If you're using a handsaw, cut into the siding with its finished face up. With a circular saw, use a carbide-tipped blade; cutting siding can dull softer metals. Always wear safety glasses or protective goggles when sawing.

7 A pair of ladder jacks helps you work securely in high places. You can rent jacks at most lumberyards. Stand two ladders side by side and attach one jack to the back of each ladder, suspending the jacks from two rungs. Lay a scaffold board between the jacks for a sturdy work platform.

To eliminate a lot of tiring climbing up and down, divide your work crew into separate ladder and ground teams. The ladder team can measure and nail, while the ground crew cuts the siding and carries it to the installation site. If you want to divide labor equally among crew members, switch jobs each time you raise the ladder jacks.

8 You'll need to measure extremely accurately to fit siding around door and window frames and other openings. If you've removed the old siding, use pieces of it as templates. Otherwise, make a paper template, then transfer the contour to the back or front of the siding, depending on the type of saw you're using.

Wood, metal, or vinyl drip caps installed over door and window openings help protect frames from water damage. If you don't install drip caps, place shims behind the siding to angle it outward and direct water runoff away from door and window frames.

9 When all the siding has been installed, caulk around doors and windows and alongside the corner boards. The caulk buffer allows the siding to expand and contract without buckling. Many siding manufacturers make color-matched caulk and prefinished nails to go with their products, or you can buy acrylic caulk in a wide variety of tints.

To install exterior lights and other fixtures, first drill holes at the corners of where you want the openings to be, then make cutouts by sawing from one hole to the next with a keyhole or saber saw. Caulk around the edge of the opening before reinstalling the fixture. Tuck phone and television antenna lines along the shadow lines of courses to make them less visible.

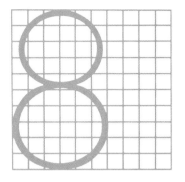

8

PORCHES, PATIOS, DECKS, AND STOOPS

No matter where you live, there are bound to be at least a few months of the year when you and your family practically live outdoors. Porches, patios, decks, and stoops are, at their best, outdoor living rooms that combine all the comforts of home with the fresh air and freedom of the great outdoors. Even in bad weather, certain outdoor areas of your home—entries and gates, for example—capture attention and serve as transitions from indoors to outdoors. Let this chapter serve as an idea resource to help you put your outdoor spaces to the most enjoyable and most attractive use.

THE OUTSIDE ENTRY

Even if you haven't planned it that way, an outside front entry gives visitors their first impression of your home. With a little creativity, thought, and work, that first look can be very impressive.

The intriguing entry pictured *at right,* for example, frames the front door and leaves no doubt that this is the entrance for guests. It acts as a frame within a frame, with the garden walls and double row of evergreens delineating the ruler-straight front path.

This outdoor entry also is practical: Thanks to its shadow-box design, it shelters the door from the elements to some extent. In a wet or cold climate, however, you'd need an enclosed air-lock entry.

An outside entry can take many other forms, of course. Here are just a few additional possibilities.
• Consider using fencing to frame the path and separate public and private areas; fencing also can block your view of parked cars.
• For a quick change of direction, lead the eye—and foot—to the front door with an instant hedge made of shrubs in planters.
• Ask yourself if your house would benefit from a purely decorative entry feature, such as an arbor or lath roof framing the front door. Whether traditional or contemporary in design, this type of addition can add lots of charm to any home, with relatively little effort and expense.
• If you think a more ambitious project is in order, think about adding a full-fledged enclosed vestibule to a house. Not only will it make an appealing entry, it also will cut down on energy loss and costs.

GATEWAYS

Gateways, too, are outside entries, though they're at least a step removed from the house itself. They should be inviting, but not *too* inviting. Gateways mark the transition from public to private areas, guide visitors in, and should keep casual intruders out. A gate and its accompanying fence, whatever their design and material, can be both useful and beautiful.

The three gates shown here each separate various outdoor areas from each other, but that's about all they have in common.

The airy-looking grillwork gate pictured *at upper right* leads to a patio that is fenced for privacy. The warm tones of the cedar fence blend with the house itself, and the grillwork of the gate adds interest to the home's simple shape.

The strongly vertical lines of the board gate and fence shown *at lower right* both contrast with and complement the traditional lapped siding of the home they adjoin. The gate keeps the backyard private, without completely blocking views in and out.

The dramatic arched gate pictured *opposite* serves as a graceful entry to the yard of a traditionally styled shingle-sided house. Only when the gate is partially open, as it is here, are tantalizing glimpses of the deck, trellis, front door, and path available to those on the other side of the fence.

Practical considerations

Although ready-made gates are available, you may decide that a custom-made or home-made gate will suit your needs best. Here are some points to consider when you're planning to purchase a gate or its components.

• Look for sturdy, weather-resistant hinges and latches.

• Be sure the gate is at least an inch narrower than the gateway opening, so it can swing freely.

• Proportion is very important. A gate that is too small for its adjacent fence will look puny and ineffective; one that is too high will seem forbidding and institutional. Do some sketches and let your eye be the judge, or borrow the dimensions of a favorite existing gate.

THE FRONT PORCH

After a generation of houses with outdoor living focused on the backyard, front porches are making a comeback. A front porch provides a place the whole family, and neighbors as well, can enjoy. It doesn't have to be elaborate, but certain features are indispensable: A well-chosen floor provides a solid, nonskid surface for rocking chairs and gliders; a sound roof keeps out rain and sun and holds up the porch swing; and open sides not only let breezes flow through but also allow for a good view of the world outside.

The full-width porch shown *at left* was added to a house that previously had not boasted any porch. Thirty-six feet long and 6 feet deep, the new porch adds distinction to the home's exterior and creates a delightful family gathering place. An additional benefit, not part of the original plan, is the cool shade the home's front rooms now enjoy in the heat of the summer.

Practical considerations

Most families will need the services of a contractor and perhaps an architect to add a porch to their home. Whether you expect to have professional assistance or hope to do the job yourself, several points must be considered.

• Porches can be placed almost at ground level on a flat lot, although on a sloping site you may require several steps to bring the porch up to the level of the rest of your home. No matter what its height, block or poured-concrete wall footings at the perimeter will support the porch. The footings should extend below the frost line. Check that excavation for the supports will not disturb underground utilities or tree roots.

• Polyethylene film laid on the earth beneath the porch will act as a vapor barrier and keep the crawl space clean and dry.

• Find out before you start work whether you need a building permit. Check other building regulations, too, such as local setback requirements.

• Plan for easy access to the porch from the main living area of your home. You may be able to take advantage of an existing door, but don't hesitate to provide a new doorway if that will make a better traffic pattern.

THE BACK PORCH

Everything a front porch can do, a back porch can, too, with one exception: With a back porch, you exchange some degree of neighborhood sociability for privacy. In most houses, a back porch is more likely than a front porch to be adjacent to the kitchen and convenient to the barbecue area. Thus, it's an ideal outdoor dining and family room, and lends itself to summertime entertaining as well. At its simplest and perhaps its best, a back porch is a great spot for watching nightfall when the fireflies begin to twinkle. If you don't have a back porch, the one featured here may inspire you to build one; if you do have a back porch, here are some new ways to make use of it.

The back porch shown *above* and *at right* adds architectural interest to a house that once had little to set it apart from its neighbors. Better still, the 8x30-foot addition has become a favorite place for summertime gathering and cooling off.

The porch's materials integrate it perfectly with the house. Asphalt roof shingles match those of the main house; the narrow triangular wall section below the roof was sided and painted to match the house; and the porch railing and trim were painted white to coordinate with the home's trim. Sand-colored quarry tile on the porch floor blends well with the brick walls, and the ceiling, made of plywood with molding strips at the seams, is painted white to make the porch seem brighter and more cheerful.

Furnishing a porch
Because this house is located in a dry, mild climate, the owners needn't worry about strong wind and rain ruining the wood

furniture they use on the porch. In addition, the deep roof overhang provides enough protection so that during infrequent storms the furniture can be pushed up against the back wall.

If you live in a less kindly climate, plan your porch furnishings accordingly. Be sure that finishes are moisture-resistant and materials not susceptible to sun damage and changes in temperature and humidity. Consider purchasing covers to protect your investment during inclement weather.

Another good feature of this porch is the central step, which divides the space into two well-defined seating areas. Adults can visit or relax in one half while, in the other section, youngsters concentrate on games.

THE SCREENED PORCH

Day and night, screened porches invite you to linger outdoors. In daytime, you enjoy both the shade and the view. In the evening, you enjoy the freedom from insects that only screens can provide. During heat waves, a screened porch may even prove to be the most comfortable place around, short of a swimming pool or an air-conditioned room. In short, a screened porch is an old-fashioned amenity that still has great appeal to homeowners.

The 8x24-foot screened porch featured here was added to the back of a vintage suburban house to provide informal space for dining, play, and entertaining.

In keeping with the rest of the home, the porch is traditional in style, its railing painted white to match the trim of the main house. Gracefully turned spindles painted a soft brown offer period charm. The porch floor is tongue-and-groove fir, painted a light beige to reflect as much light as possible; the white-painted ceiling is made of car siding. Wicker furniture sends out an irresistible invitation to sit down and relax in nostalgic comfort.

On a practical note, the screening is attached to frames outside the porch railings. This protects the screens from rough-and-tumble goings-on inside, and makes them easily accessible for repairs if any damage does occur.

Although this porch is located at the back of the house, a screened porch can be at home anywhere—front, back, side, or even wrapped around a corner. Much depends on the floor plan of your home and the shape and size of your lot.

Orientation to the sun is a key consideration, too. For example, most houses don't need more shade on the north side, but additional shade might well be appreciated on a southern exposure—provided heat buildup in late afternoons doesn't keep you off the porch.

If overheating is a problem, consider using a ceiling fan to cool the area. You might also want to switch to solar screening. Made of fiberglass or aluminum mesh, solar screening looks much like ordinary screening, but the material is thicker and specially woven to minimize solar heat gain.

THE PATIO

Patios take the prize for ground-level versatility. If you have a flat strip of land, or one that can be made flat, you can build a patio. What's more, most patios are less complex to build than porches, and sometimes less expensive than decks, depending on the surfacing material you choose. Patios take full advantage of the sun, air, and view, yet can be shaded by trellises, canopies, or even trees. They're ideal for entertaining, and for unwinding. You might even decide to build two patios, one adjacent to the family room, another, protected by a fence or hedge, opening out from the master bedroom.

A perfect patio comes in many forms. It can be square, rectangular, or even free-form. It can be paved with sand-set brick, flagstone, or concrete. It may boast a gracious floor of tile or a rustic base of wood rounds. Even pebbles make a good patio if they're carefully raked and contained by curbing.

The patio pictured *at right* features hexagonal paving tile flooring in a terra-cotta color that harmonizes with the home's mission tile roof. White curbing and a low retaining wall match the house's stucco exterior.

If you're planning a new patio, consider traffic patterns into and out of the house, as well as to other areas of the yard. Make the patio convenient, but don't place it at a crossroad.

Also study how much light the area gets at different times of day and year. In spring, full sunlight may be welcome, but in August, you'll need some type of shade. This can be achieved in various ways.

Trees are the obvious shade source—they needn't be very large to provide sufficient shade. Your house itself also may cast a cool shadow over the patio. Or you can build a roof overhang to shelter part of the patio, or use canvas awnings or split bamboo for handsome and movable shading. The most portable type of screen, of course, is the classic umbrella, either freestanding or attached to a picnic table. Lathing, translucent fiberglass, and plastic are other possibilities.

To extend the patio season, consider adding attractive outdoor lighting and a portable heating system. These can make a big difference on a mild early-spring night or a cool but brilliant autumn day.

PORCHES, PATIOS, DECKS, AND STOOPS

DECKS

Is your lot too hilly for a porch or patio? Build a deck to bring outdoor living to your doorstep. Is your soil unsuited for gardening or your garden area too far from the house? Bedecked with planters, a deck can put vegetables, herbs, or flowers within easy reach. You can add a deck upstairs, downstairs, or even free-standing in the middle of the yard. Any place a deck will work at your house offers almost unbeatable potential for added outdoor living space.

The deck pictured *at right* really is two decks. Its upper level is a full story above grade; halfway down, a second deck frames a hot tub and screened gazebo; at the bottom of the stairs, a patio, shaded by the deck above, provides a cool, sheltered spot to sit on too-hot days.

Check the inset photo *opposite* and you can see how the decks' geometric shapes complement the home's angles. The upper deck juts out from a triangular bay window, and the middle level hooks around the gazebo, which is tucked into a corner to avoid blocking the lake view from above.

Sheltered from drafts by the house, the mid-level deck lets the homeowners enjoy the hot tub from early spring to late fall. Because of its elevation, the tub also commands a view of the lake.

Distinctive finishing touches add even more livability. Custom-designed light fixtures extend the decks' usability into the evening hours. Flowers in built-in planters add color and charm to the setting.

Decks harmonize best with contemporary-style houses, but with careful siting and scaling you can plan one that won't look out of place on a traditional home.

A project as complex as the one featured here would almost certainly require the design and construction assistance of an architect and/or contractor. But a deck need not be lavish. For example, space atop a porch or attached garage might be perfect—and easily adapted—for a bedroom deck. Or several small decks might offer a luxurious but affordable alternative to one showplace deck. For tips about building decks, see the next two pages.

(continued)

DECKS
(continued)

Before you start work on a deck, check zoning regulations, easements, and building codes. Then start planning. Keep in mind that you should allow at least 20 square feet of floor space for each person expected to use the deck. Whatever their size and configuration, most decks fall into a few basic categories, as illustrated *below*.

• A *grade-level deck* will work with just about any type of house. It's the simplest to build and takes nicely to embellishments such as planters or decorative railings.

• A *raised deck* suits a house whose main level is above grade. A deck of this type also can be extended out from an upstairs room in a two-story or split-entry home.

• A *bi-level deck* features, as the name implies, two recreation and relaxing areas. Besides offering the potential for two activities to coexist peacefully, a bi-level deck makes an easy transition from a high deck to ground level.

Where you choose to locate a deck depends not only on access from the indoors and where you have the space, but also on climate. In warm regions, you'll want to build on the cooler sides of the house—the north and east. In cool climates, the south and west sides of the home will be warmer in spring and fall, extending the season you can enjoy the deck.

The compact deck pictured *at right* features not only a small sitting area and a container garden, but a hot tub, too. Surrounded by warm-climate plantings, the deck offers its owners an instant resort-style vacation as soon as they step out their back door.

DECK TYPES

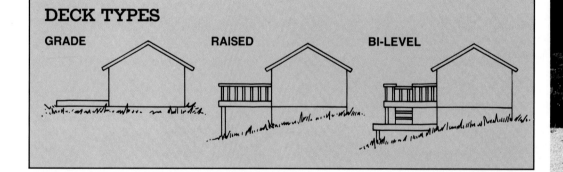

GRADE **RAISED** **BI-LEVEL**

CHOOSING DECK MATERIALS

To build a deck, use only wood that can withstand the weather. Suitable species include redwood, cedar, cypress, pressure-treated lumber (fir is most common), and exterior-grade plywood. For parts of the deck that don't touch the ground, you can use untreated lumber coated with preservative; be sure to treat all sawed edges and nail holes.

• *Redwood heartwood* is almost impervious to attack by the elements. If you are using less-resistant *sapwood,* apply penetrating-oil stain/

sealer for added protection.

• *Cedar* and *cypress,* often sold with rough surfaces, can be left unfinished, but you can stain them if you prefer. Both are naturally rot-resistant; they are somewhat stronger than redwood, and less costly.

• Not all *pressure-treated wood* can be stained or painted, so check this before you buy.

No matter what type of deck you decide to build, the basic materials will be much the same. The deck surface will be made of either 2x4s

or 2x6s. You also can use exterior-grade plywood sealed at the joints and covered with waterproof silicone deck coating. Be sure to seal all edges of the plywood either with other lumber or by caulking all joints.

Joists should be 2x10s, attached by joist hangers to a 2x12 ledger through-bolted to the side of the house. As always, when working on outside structures, be sure all nails and other hardware you use are galvanized to inhibit rusting.

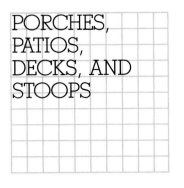
STOOPS

A stoop may seem like an odd name for something that delivers you *up* to a door. But it makes sense once you learn that the name is derived from the Dutch word for step. And that's the nature of the stoop: It's a small platform reached by a few steps. Few houses are built directly on grade, and a stoop conquers the problem of getting from ground to door. If there is a small roof overhead, the stoop also provides shelter from rain when you open the door or step out to get your mail. In urban areas, where houses are built right up to the sidewalk, a stoop makes a handy, pocket-size front porch.

Stoops can show up many places outside a house—at the front entry, at the back door, or at a side service entrance. The standard small concrete stoop, however, often is too cramped to serve as anything more than a transitional platform; expanded and/or modified, it can become more useful, and more attractive, too.

The small wood deck in the photo *above* is a case in point. Here, a new wood structure was built and extended right over the original concrete stoop. A ledger board anchored at the house and 4x4 posts at the corners support joists and decking. The steps are 2x4s nailed on edge.

Now there's plenty of room to maneuver, even with groceries or a toddler in hand. And planning ahead for the social aspects of stoop-sitting, these owners included built-in benches in their project. A simple design of this type could be dressed up even more with added amenities such as planters or a trellis.

Structurally, you can deal with a stoop in one of several different ways. You can demolish the entire stoop (an arduous task) and start over again. An easier alternative is to retain the original concrete platform, but remove the steps, as the owners of the stoop shown *above* did. Or you can build over everything, steps and all. Whichever way you choose, make sure the new floor level will not interfere with an outswinging storm door.

The gracious outdoor living area pictured *at right* also started out as an ordinary stoop, but was expanded with considerably more decking than the version shown above. Extending an already-deep eave and adding a trellis for climbing vines created more shelter for the entry. The trellis also helps separate traffic in and out of the house from a seating area at right. Wide steps from the driveway angle in two directions: to the front door and to the bench-seating area.

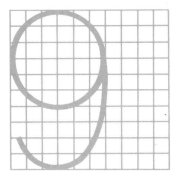

IMPROVING OUTDOOR LIVING

Remodeling doesn't always have to be an inside job. If shadeless surroundings, a paltry patio, or a diminutive deck is cramping the outdoor living at your house, maybe you should remodel your yard. One of the best things about improving outdoor living space is that you don't have to tear up everything and start all over again. Instead, you can develop a design that lets you build upon what's already there. Do the work one step at a time, and you also can get it all done without demolishing your budget. This chapter tells—and shows—how.

PLANNING OUTDOOR LIVING AREAS

Whether you're thinking about a multilevel deck expansion or just a couple of new built-in benches, careful planning is the key to getting the most out of outdoor living spaces.

Before you do any remodeling, or even proceed into the planning stages, check with your local building department: Ask about zoning ordinances, lot restrictions, and building codes that may affect your project. Also, be sure to find out whether your property deed limits outdoor development of your lot.

Next, take inventory of your yard's assets and liabilities. Think about how existing landscaping, fencing, and walkways can be incorporated into your overall plan. Evaluate options that might help reduce your home's energy bills, such as planting quick-growing trees or large shrubs to provide shade in hot weather.

Now devote some time to daydreaming about your "perfect" yard. Balance your fantasies against your budget and available space, and start putting your ideas on paper. If your backyard doesn't seem big enough for all you have planned, consider expanding into a side yard; even the front yard may be usable in some circumstances.

Make sure you allot plenty of room for your family to stretch out and relax, barbecue, and entertain. Consider privacy and access. If you're planning to expand a patio or deck, don't restrict your design to squares and rectangles. Try setting a patio or deck extension at an interesting angle to the existing surface.

Finally, before you completely commit yourself to any project, check the suitability and practicality of your ideas by staking out a full-size, ground-level plan, as shown *opposite*.

To do this you'll need stakes, heavy-duty cord, a long (50-foot) measuring tape, a mason's line level, and perhaps a framing square. Sharpen a point on an end of each stake and drive one into the ground at each corner of the patio or deck you envision, and also at intermediate points on long runs.

If you like what you see, run cord from stake to stake, then step into your proposed new outdoor area and move around in it. Is there enough room for the furniture or other items, such as a barbecue grill, that you'd like to use out here? How about traffic patterns? How closely will the new structure encroach upon existing plantings, especially trees?

Finalizing your plan

Once you're satisfied with the perimeters, it's time to square up the corners and level the lines. Use a framing square at the corners or, better yet, check them with the 3-4-5 method. To do this, measure and mark 3 feet along one leg of a corner, 4 feet along the other; if the diagonal distance between the two points is 5 feet, the corner is square. To assure that an entire area is square, also measure diagonal distances from opposite corners; if the diagonals are equal in length, the area is square.

Hang the line level from the cord at various points and check for level. If you're planning an above-grade deck, as the owner in the photograph *opposite* did, situate the cord at the height the new deck will be.

CREATING PRIVACY

If you feel as though you're on stage every time you grill a few hamburgers or stretch out on a lawn chair, the outdoor living at your house lacks one key ingredient—privacy. Maybe all you need is some additional shrubbery or an open-work trellis that masks but doesn't obliterate a less-than-attractive view. Or perhaps you should think about your entire yard as an outdoor room that needs walls around it. Whatever the privacy problems outside your house, here are some important points to consider.

P rivacy is a matter of degrees. This means that in assessing your outdoor living, you need to determine just how much privacy you really need. Do you want total separation from neighboring yards, or would you be better off with a simple rail fence that merely defines boundaries for the eye? Is noise or wind a problem? How about fencing in pets or small children?

The pint-size, 30x25-foot space pictured *at right* exemplifies a nearly total approach to creating privacy. Though the space is boxed in by neighboring houses, a careful combination of materials and a well-thought-out "floor plan" have turned it into an alfresco family room, with areas for dining, relaxing, even gardening. Here, solid fencing and an overhead trellis work together to provide a sense of seclusion without impeding good air circulation. Vines, shrubs, and small trees soften the strong vertical lines of the fences, and potted plants add touches of color.

Peekaboo privacy
In many cases, you might not want or need anything as opaque as a tall, solid fence. Instead, you could choose staggered boards or some other open-work fencing material to partially shield you from view and let breezes cool your yard. Hedges, thick and dense, serve as living fences. Even a few well-placed bushes can block views from the street or the yard next door.

Consider, for example, the backyard kitchen (it's complete with a gas grill, small refrigerator, and stainless steel bar sink) shown *above*. Behind the cook center, a mature hedge and white latticework create privacy from the house and driveway next door.

(continued)

CREATING PRIVACY
(continued)

When you select the "walls" that will define and shelter outdoor living spaces, consider the appearance of the materials you have in mind, as well as the degree of privacy they offer. It's important that the materials complement, and if possible improve upon, your home's exterior appearance. If the fence will be visible from the street, also give some thought to how it will fit into the character of your neighborhood.

With the outdoor living area in the backyard pictured *at left*, appearances were a prime consideration. The homeowners started out with a run-of-the-mill back stoop and a featureless yard. Now a multilevel deck is the center of attention. Originally, an old-fashioned picket fence had separated this yard from the one next door. It was replaced with an updated version that assures plenty of privacy and adds to the charm of both yards at the same time.

Practical matters
The sturdiness of a fence is determined largely by the support posts you use. For a wood fence, posts should be at least 4x4s, planted firmly in the ground, in concrete, and below the frost line; space the posts about 6 feet apart. The belowground surfaces of fence posts should be treated with a wood preservative, unless the posts are cut from redwood, cedar, or pressure-treated lumber.

Fencing alternatives
As this photo shows, classic wood fences have lots of charm as well as lots of privacy potential. Other materials are popular for fencing, too, although they may lack the warmth and versatility of wood. Chain-link and welded-wire fences, for example, do a good job of containing children and pets and require less maintenance than most wood fences; to soften metal fencing's industrial look and make it more private, weave colored plastic slats through the fence.

Walls and fences of brick or stone, although costly to install, add greatly to the appeal of most homes. If your yard is spacious enough, masonry walls can provide maximum privacy without an uncomfortably closed-in look. Plantings, too, combine charm with practicality. For screening, rather than solid-wall-style privacy, moderate-size evergreens or flowering shrubs can give almost instant results. If you live in a heavily trafficked area, consider using an earth berm or thick shrubbery to muffle street noise.

Whatever materials you use, be sure to plan the placement of all the elements of your outdoor remodeling for everyday use, not just for peace, quiet, and visual privacy. Always allow for easy access to your house, yard, driveway, and street. See pages 136–139 for more about this.

CREATING SHADE

Providing shelter from the sun offers a dramatic way to change the character of your whole yard, and the sky's the limit on ways you can put outdoor living space in the shade. Trellises, roof overhangs, fences, and other simple structures can keep you and your home cool on hot days. Plants and trees also can fill the bill. Or combine both structural and growing things for your own special place out of the sun.

Before you build or plant anything, think about which parts of your home and yard you want to screen and what time of the day you need shade. Shading on the south side of your house, for example, should be almost completely overhead, because this area probably gets sun almost all day. In contrast, a sun screen on the west side should block low, late-afternoon sun.

If you live in an area where hot sun could cause heat to build up under structural shading, roof it with materials such as lath, movable canvas, or evenly spaced boards that let heat escape. On the sun screen pictured *at right*, for example, 2x2s nailed to rafter extensions allow air to circulate and cast striped shadows on the decking underneath. A screened porch at the left of the photo provides total relief from the sun and also shades a hot tub most of the day.

Shading with nature

Trees not only block sunlight, they also create visual interest and places for birds to take up residence. Deciduous trees make sense in most parts of the country, because they cast shade only in late spring, summer, and early fall; once deciduous trees lose their leaves, they don't interfere with welcome winter sunshine. For quick results, choose fast-growing softwood trees such as weeping willow, silver maple, gray birch, or Chinese elm. If you're planning for the future, select slower-growing but longer-lived hardwoods such as sugar maple or oak.

And don't ignore the shade possibilities of fast-growing vines. Different types thrive in different climates and soils, so order carefully from catalogs or a local garden center.

IMPROVING OUTDOOR LIVING

REVAMPING AN ENTIRE YARD

If you're thinking about adding, extending, or improving outdoor living, consider the big picture. What would a new deck, patio—or a combination of them— do for your home's environs? Take landscaping into account, too; maybe just a few changes could make your entire yard work better. Here and on pages 138–139 are examples of successful transformations that just might inspire you to begin looking at your whole yard in a different way.

The multi-decked yard pictured *at right* came about when the owners decided to add a room to the back of their house. This meant cutting down the backyard to just 25x40 feet. Rethinking and reorganizing the entire area resulted in a scheme that makes the most of every square foot.

Check the plan *below,* and you can see that a cedar deck angles away from the house, improving access from the side yard. A short bridge connects the deck to a brick patio. Built-in planters and benches make the most of peripheral sections of the yard, and boulder-strewn landscaping eliminates lawn-mowing chores.

Even if your yard isn't going to be affected by an interior remodeling that works its way outside, you may well want to think about subdividing outdoor spaces. Setting aside small, separate places for specific functions such as sunning, sitting, eating, or entertaining can make your lot seem a lot larger. *(continued)*

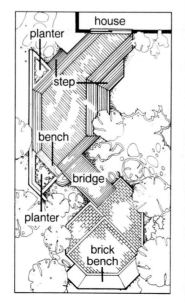

REVAMPING AN ENTIRE YARD
(continued)

Originally, the home pictured *at right* just had a small deck, accessible only through sliding glass doors from the family room. Now a second-stage deck, one step lower than the first, wraps almost all the way around the back of the house. The new decking and rocks around its perimeter take advantage of a shady setting where grass once refused to grow.

Adding on to most patios or decks usually isn't a costly proposition, and most of the work involved can be done by a weekend do-it-yourselfer. Big landscaping jobs can be arduous, though; you might want to contract some or all of them to a nursery, or do the work yourself in stages spread over several years.

With materials in a whole-yard scheme, you can be as creative as you please, mixing or matching new and old materials. You might choose, for instance, to extend a brick patio with a fieldstone L, or add an angled-board deck to a straight-line original.

Changes in elevation offer another good way to add interest, and possibly solve problems as well. For example, think about terracing a steeply sloping yard with multilevel decks that step up or down from the original, or stack a deck over a patio and get two levels of outdoor living in the space of one.

If you're satisfied with the *amount* of outdoor space your home offers but still feel something's missing, consider adding a small luxury or two, such as a firepit, built-in benches and tables for outdoor meals, or a corner gazebo. The following pages take you through a yard full of luxuries that developed in a series of six stages.

DEVELOPING
A YARD
IN STAGES

There are several good reasons to plan and develop your yard a step at a time. Money, or rather a lack of it, is the most obvious, of course. Developing an entire yard can be costly. More subtle, but still very important, is experience. You don't necessarily know what you want as soon as you move into a home, and making changes one at a time gives you chances to launch your ideas, see which ones fly, and use the successful projects as taking-off points for others. The backyard remodeling featured here and on the following pages exemplifies staged development at its best.

STAGE 1

bar

upper deck

shade structure

stairs

Starting with a backyard that was bare except for an avocado tree, the owner of this lushly landscaped and wonderfully livable yard developed a master plan before he turned the first shovelful of earth. After planning the layout and all the structures on his own, he contracted out the actual construction, landscaping, and installation over a period of several years. The result, a multilevel recreation and entertainment space, lives up to all his expectations.

As you can see in the plan *above*, Stage 1 of the project involved turning a flat roof over part of the home's lower level into a 30x15-foot fenced-in deck.

This deck, in finished, completely furnished form, is pictured *at right*. With access from the second-floor living room, and a stairway that leads to the yard, this redwood refuge is ideal for entertaining.

Freestanding benches can be rearranged as needed for seating. Lattice walls provide privacy and safety, and cutouts in the back wall offer a commanding view of the yard below.

Other intriguing details include recycled cornice pieces from a demolished mortuary, a portable bar, and a canvas-topped shade structure at one end.

Good looks and entertaining weren't the only considerations here. The decking was constructed from 1x4 redwood in sections that can be removed easily to maintain the roof underneath.

(continued)

DEVELOPING
A YARD
IN STAGES
(continued)

Stage 2 of this whole-yard project included the spa and garden shed pictured *opposite*. The homeowner installed the 4x6-foot acrylic spa as close to the house as possible. Because neighbors on that side of the yard would have had a bird's-eye view of the spa, the owner designed a two-story enclosure with a striped canvas shade on top that can easily be lowered when the spa is in use. A gate below the shade leads to the side yard.

A 12x15-foot garden shed adjacent to the spa provides lots of room for spa equipment, garden tools, and extra outdoor furniture, as well as facilities for repotting the abundance of plants that give the whole yard so much charm. The shed is roofed with planks so guests on the upper-level deck (see Stage 4, discussed below and on page 144) can't look in on the equipment. Inside the shed, a flagstone floor, a wall of storage shelves, and a simple overhead lighting system finish the work area.

In Stage 3, the center of the yard was covered with a 24x24-foot redwood shade structure, shown *at upper right*. Supported by six hefty 6x6 posts bolted to metal brackets set in concrete, the framework is very durable. Overhead crossbeams at the front and back of the unit sandwich lighting and its wiring between pairs of 2x12s. Wisteria planted around the perimeter of the sun screen will eventually cover it, supplementing the shade provided by the structure itself.

In Stage 4, redwood decks surrounding the central sun screen were constructed. The large photo on pages 144 and 145 shows a close-up of one of these decks.

(continued)

STAGES 2, 3, & 4

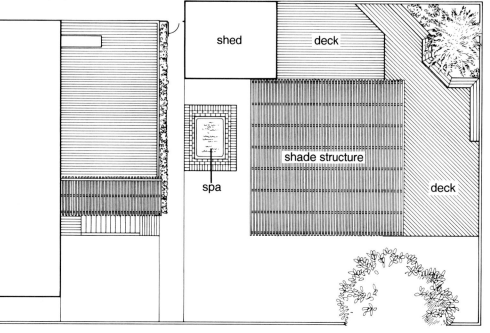

shed | deck
spa
shade structure
deck

DEVELOPING A YARD IN STAGES

(continued)

To accommodate a slight slope in the yard, the Stage 4 decks pictured *at far right* were built on two levels. The deck next to the garden shed is two steps up from the bricked area and is used primarily as an eating area; the other deck is three steps up and is used for sunning and relaxing. Built-in redwood benches follow the perimeter of the decks.

The final two phases of the yard project concentrated on filling in some blanks. In Stage 5, the remaining areas, including the floor under the shade structure, perimeter walkways, and a small patio in one corner, were bricked. At the same time, low masonry walls were put up to define planting beds around the yard's perimeter. In addition, a Mexican fountain was installed. Encircled by greenery, it adds the music of flowing water. Light fixtures placed at strategic intervals around the yard enhance the beauty and usability of all the spaces at night.

In Stage 6, the homeowner created a quiet, secluded spot for reading and reflection. He used the far corner of the yard as a setting for a triangular shelter shown *at upper near right.* There had been an old and broken-down lath fence in this corner; it was replaced with redwood fencing that matches the rest of the yard's enclosures.

A previously completed brick planter supports the back edges of the bench; overhead, the redwood sun screen mirrors the detailing of the other sun-control structures in the yard. Shade-loving plants add to the garden-paradise mood.

Incidentally, there may be a Stage 7. The owner is considering adding a gazebo on the brick patio in the right rear corner of the yard.

STAGES 5 & 6

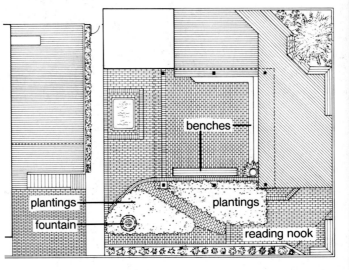

benches

plantings

plantings

fountain

reading nook

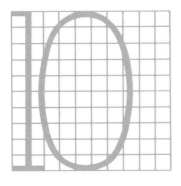

TOOLS, TASKS, & TECHNIQUES

Keeping up your home's exterior and surroundings usually is a year-round task, no matter where you live. Whatever the age, condition, and landscape style of your home, some seasonal maintenance tasks are constants. This chapter can help you choose the tools and equipment you'll need for seasonal chores, show you how to keep them in good working order, and offer some suggestions about how to cope with the effects of nature's temperament on your home.

Because the tools you use outside your home have to withstand rugged use and more-than-occasional abuse, it pays to buy the best you can afford. Good-quality tools last for years with only occasional care.

If you're starting from scratch, you'll be able to get along with a basic set of tools, to which you can add as needs arise. Which tools you need right away depend upon how much you'll be doing outside your home. If you plan to hire someone to do much of the work, you'll need relatively few tools of your own. And if you have a small, vinyl-sided home with a miniature yard and few plantings, your maintenance and tool needs obviously will be less than they would be for a large clapboard home surrounded by extensive plantings, many trees, and a sizable garden.

Cost probably is the first thing you'll wonder about when you consider buying tools for the first time. If you're willing to pay about $100, you can buy lawn and garden tools that are made of polished stainless steel and unbreakable handles and come with lifetime guarantees. Good, serviceable tools, however, can be purchased for a fraction of that cost and, with proper handling, should last nearly as long as more expensive tools.

Tools with handles
Long-handle tools, such as hoes, shovels, and forks, should have "working" ends of one-piece forged steel. They'll hold up longer than ones with two or more parts welded together. Don't let a nice coat of paint on the metal parts fool you—a brightly painted finish may conceal welds or manufacturing flaws and the paint will soon wear off anyway.

Handles, too, must be tough and fault-free, since they carry the force you exert to the working end. Better tools have finely turned handles of strong yet resilient hardwood, such as hickory. Inspect handles closely for grain direction—it should run with the length and be well-defined. Watch for knots, checks, and other possible interruptions of grain. These are potential weak points that will break under strain. For this reason, never buy a tool with a painted handle; you won't be able to see the wood's grain. The manufacturer-applied finish should be smooth to the touch and scratch-free, or you'll develop blisters every time you use the tool. The factory finish won't last forever under constant use, but the handle can be resanded and refinished when necessary.

Tools with handles pose a special problem: The handles have a tendency to work loose and come off if they're not properly attached. Choose tools with the best possible connection between handle and working end. All long-handle tools have sockets on the metal end; these accept the tapered handle for a forced friction fit. For extra security, some manufacturers add screws through the metal into the wood. The combination of a tight friction fit and the screws makes for long wear.

All the quality considerations that apply for long-handle tools apply to small, short-handle tools, as well. Hand trowels, forks, and small planting spades should be either of all-metal one-piece construction or fitted with strong, comfortable wood handles that won't come loose. Avoid tools with plastic handles—they won't have the necessary strength.

Cutting tools
Besides the assortment of hoes, shovels, forks, trowels, and other digging and raking tools, you'll need some specialized cutting tools for outdoor tasks.

Shears—small ones for grass and larger ones for bushes and light branches—should be of tool steel, comfortable to hold and sturdily constructed. The back-and-forth cutting action must be efficient, and as effortless as possible. Look for grass shears with a spring action that returns them to position after each clip.

Pruning and limbing saws, to do the best job, should feature tempered steel blades and a handle of either hardwood or ABS plastic; either must be easy to grasp and hold. The handle should be attached to the blade securely, normally with three or more seated screws. Saws with a non-binding feature—extra, angled teeth—cost more but are worth the price.

Also handy to have around is a hatchet, a small ax, or both. Generally, the guidelines for long-handle tools apply to these, as well. Choose a strong, well-fitted handle and a tempered tool-steel head that will take a sharp edge and hold it. Consider the balance and feel of the tool in your hands. Though more expensive, hatchets and small axes of one-piece forged steel last a lifetime.

Which tools to buy?
The following list will give you an idea of the basic tools you'll need for outdoor chores. You'll discover many more in hardware stores and tool catalogs.

Many of those mentioned here serve more than one purpose and are particularly useful for that reason. Tools marked with an asterisk (*) are nice to have but not among the first you should buy; add them to your collection gradually, as needs arise or funds become available.

• *For the lawn*
18- to 20-inch-cut
   walking mower
Spring-type lawn rake
Bow rake
Grass shears
Oscillating sprinkler
50-foot (minimum)
   garden hose
Square-blade border spade
Lawn edger*
Grass thatcher*
Two-wheel garden cart or
   wheelbarrow*
Fertilizer spreader*
Weed sprayer*

• *For the garden*
Round-pointed shovel
Hoe
Digging fork
Digging spade
Hand tools—trowel,
   fork, planter
Hand cultivator*

• *For trees and shrubs*
Pruning shears for small
   branches
Lopping shears for large
   branches*
Pruning saw
Pole saw for high trimming*
Hatchet or small ax
10-foot rung-type
   straight ladder
20-foot extension ladder*

• *For removing snow and ice*
Snow shovel
Ice chipper
Roof rake*

There's no doubt that power equipment makes most outdoor tasks easier. But power tools have their disadvantages—noise and maintenance are the most obvious—as well as their advantages, so make choices accordingly.

The first piece of outdoor power equipment most homeowners buy is a lawn mower. There's little on the negative side here—a power mower does a neater, faster job and requires less physical exertion than the human-powered type (although if your lawn is very small, a power mower may not be worthwhile). The main question is what kind of power mower to buy—gas or electric, self-propelled or push-type, rider or walk-behind.

Once you decide to buy a power mower, here are some points to keep in mind.

• Unless you'll be mowing lawns for profit, having a mower that's larger than you need is wasteful. Consult the salesperson about the size needed for your lawn.

• A smaller mower is easier than a large one to maneuver around trees and along hedges. Choose a mower that will minimize the need to hand-trim.

• If your lawn is relatively small and unobstructed, you might also consider a quiet electric mower with a heavy-duty extension cord.

• A self-propelled mower can be dangerous for an inexperienced operator. It also deprives you of exercise.

• The more belts, options, shifts, and adjustments a mower has, the more maintenance and repair it's likely to need.

Other equipment
For any job that can be done with a hand tool, there's a mechanized approach, too. Here's a sampling.

• *Leaf blower.* This pushes leaves and other outdoor debris out of the way, partially replacing the time-honored rake. Gas models are very noisy, but more powerful than electric ones.

• *Power lawn sweeper.* Built like a revolving brush, this usually has a large bag attachment to catch leaves, grass clippings, pine needles, and so forth.

• *Grass and weed trimmer.* This back-saving device whips a nylon cord in a circular motion. Most are electric; the gas type is noisier, more powerful, and more costly.

• *Chain saw.* Unless you cut a great deal of wood, you don't need a chain saw. Chain saws can be dangerous in the hands of novices, and annoyingly noisy in heavily populated areas. Stick to a handsaw for limb trimming, and call an expert when necessary.

• *Snowblower.* Snow blowers are a great help if have a long path or drive and live in a snowy area.

MAINTAINING TOOLS AND EQUIPMENT

Taking care of tools and equipment is more than a way to protect your considerable investment. Good maintenance makes your seasonal work much easier. By keeping your tools and equipment in good working order, you'll eliminate a lot of the frustration that comes when something breaks or stalls in mid-job.

Start your regular maintenance routine by finding a good place to store tools. Ideal storage quarters are indoors and dry, with normal air circulation. A small section of the garage will do nicely; the basement is good for hand tools. Storage sheds where both small and large items can be kept are ideal.

In the storage area, arrange tools so they are readily accessible, but not leaning against a wall waiting to fall down or be stumbled into. Cover power equipment to protect it against airborne dirt and accidental spills of paint. Garden hoses and electrical extension cords should be coiled and held with string or twist-ties, then hung from a hook to prevent snarling.

Lawn and garden chemicals, insecticides, paint, oil, and other liquids should be kept in a securely latched cabinet out of the reach of children. Be sure to label all containers if the original label is no longer legible. Don't store gasoline for long periods of time—besides being a fire hazard, it eventually destabilizes and becomes worthless.

Once everything is organized and stored, turn your attention to maintenance, guided by the seasonal chart *at right*.

A SEASONAL CHECKLIST

FALL

Locate and gather all hand and garden tools. Clean off dirt, leaves, and other debris. After the last mowing of the season in late fall, clean grass off the mower and its blade, wipe off grease and oil, drain gasoline, drain and change oil, lubricate moving parts. Follow the same general procedures for other power equipment. Drain water from hoses, then roll them up and store them. Coil electrical extension cords. Check your snowblower, if you have one, to be sure it's operational. Examine other winter tools, such as snow shovels, roof rake, and ice chipper, and make sure they're readily accessible.

WINTER

Sharpen hand tools such as hoes, axes, and spades. Replace broken or cracked handles. Refinish worn handles by sanding and coating with linseed oil. Remove rust from working ends of tools. Inspect all tools. Check for oil drippings under power equipment; note the source of drips, if any, and repair or have them repaired. Inventory tools and plan necessary purchases.

SPRING

Test power equipment and tune up as needed. Check the condition of garden hoses and electrical extension cords. Inventory chemicals, sprays, and insecticides and purchase as needed. Test sprinklers, and repair or replace if necessary. Clean the snowblower, drain gas, drain and change oil, lubricate, and store out of the way. Repair other winter tools as needed and store them. Inspect hand tools prior to your first expected use of the season.

SUMMER

Make periodic checks of hoses and sprinklers to be sure leaks aren't wasting water. Change oil in power equipment regularly, check belt condition. Keep equipment free of dirt during periods of heavy use. Put tools away after using. Inspect and repair tools and equipment for fall.

TUNE-UP BASICS

Begin any tune-up by cleaning the equipment, ridding it of all accumulated dirt, grease, grass, and mud. It's much easier to spot a problem if you can see it; use a rag for surface dirt, one soaked in degreaser or gasoline for greasy grime.

Next, remove the top of the air cleaner and check its sponge-like filter for dirt. Clean clogged filters by washing them in gasoline, then wringing dry. Apply a few drops of standard 30-weight oil to the filter, and work it in. Wipe off all dirt inside the housing, being careful not to brush any into the carburetor. Replace the filter and reassemble.

Next, move on to the base of the carburetor and find the fuel trap. It's made of clear glass and is between the fuel line and the carburetor. Remove the fuel line and clamp it to prevent gas spillage. Take off the bowl and shake out any gas or debris, then wipe clean. Remove the fuel line clamp and check the fuel flow. Replace the bowl and any attachments.

Now turn to the spark plug seated in the engine. Remove the spark plug wire from the top of the plug, being careful not to damage the connector inside the shield. Replace a worn and dirty plug to forestall future problems. If the plug looks clean and unworn on the electrode end, check the gap for proper spacing and then reinstall.

Before you rehook the spark plug wire to the plug, see if the electrical system is working properly and sending a spark to the plug. Do this by holding the wire no more than 1/8 inch from the plug, while pulling the rewind starter. If the system is working, you'll see a small spark jump to the plug. If not, the engine could have faulty points, a problem that calls for trained assistance.

If everything seems to be in working order, start the engine and let it run to warm up. When the engine is warm, make the necessary adjustments on the carburetor and choke until it runs evenly.

Sometimes, despite regular maintenance, gas-powered lawn mowers still act up, often in the middle of a cutting. Keep the following symptoms and probable causes in mind the next time your mower sputters and dies, doesn't start, or doesn't sound right:

• *Exhaust is smoky and engine lacks power.* This could be caused by a too-rich gasoline/air mixture. Adjust the screw on the carburetor by giving it a quarter-turn counterclockwise. Another possible cause, in four-cycle engines: oil mixed in the gas. To cure this, drain the gas tank and add new fuel.

• *Engine runs in spurts.* A loose spark plug wire attachment could cause this; so could dirt in the fuel line. Also check for a clogged air filter.

• *Mower lacks power and is hard to start.* A worn or dirty spark plug could cause this. Pull, check, and replace if necessary.

• *Engine won't start.* This could result from either a worn spark plug or a loose connection on a spark plug cable.

Most owner's manuals cover troubleshooting techniques for specific models, so keep your manual as a handy reference. Don't continue to run power equipment that isn't working properly. You might damage the engine.

TOOL-SHARPENING BASICS

It's not difficult to keep tools sharp, but you'll need some specialized materials.

Sharpening stones, or *whetstones,* either natural or manufactured, put the finishing touches on fine-bladed instruments such as knives and hatchets. A medium-grain aluminum oxide stone will last for years and serve for most touch-up sharpening chores.

A *flat single-cut file,* the kind without cross-hatching, helps remove nicks and gets an edge down to the touch-up or honing stage. A wooden-handle file makes the job easier.

Any light *oil,* including cooking oil, works to lubricate surfaces as they move against each other and to "float" off the minute particles of metal.

Crocus cloth, an emery or silicon carbide sandpaper with cloth backing, has several uses. Fine 320-grit will ready an edge; coarse 80-grit grinds away rough spots. To smooth edges, wrap this special sandpaper around a palm-size wooden block.

Tools that need only rough sharpening, such as hoes or spades, can be filed in one step to an edge that will penetrate dirt. Those with built-up edges, such as knives, must be sharpened in steps.

First, remove nicks or gouges in the edge with a flat file. Don't use a grinder on tempered steel—the heat will ruin the temper. Try to even the edge or duplicate the original bevel.

With a sharpening stone spotted with oil, pass the edge back and forth along the length of the stone on one side and then the other. Keep the tool at a 15-degree angle to the stone. Four to five sweeps on each side will do for a touch-up, but you'll need more for a really dull edge. Keep the number of strokes the same for both sides.

Finish by using crocus cloth the same way as you did the stone.

REACHING HIGH PLACES

Ladders are essential equipment for dozens of outdoor jobs, from pruning limbs to changing storm windows. There are three basic types of ladders.

• *The folding ladder,* or *stepladder,* consists of two side rails with steps mounted between them. Fastened to the top with hinges are a pair of legs. When the ladder is spread to form an A-shape, it becomes a sturdy platform. A pail shelf between the rail and steps and the legs serves as a perch for materials. Made of wood or aluminum, stepladders are available in heights from 4 to 12 feet.

• *Straight ladders* fill the gap between stepladders and extension ladders (discussed below). Steps (rungs) are fastened between the side rails. Unlike stepladders, straight ladders cannot stand alone; they must be propped against a building, tree, or other support. They are generally available in either wood or aluminum, in lengths ranging from 10 to 16 feet. Longer straight ladders are available but too unwieldy to handle alone.

• *Extension ladders,* made of wood or aluminum, allow access to high places by way of a two-section ladder system that extends the top straight ladder by means of a rope and pulley system. The two ladders remain interlocked for strength and security. Wood extension ladders are heavy and difficult to extend. However, wood ladders are considered safer when working near electrical wires and they flex less than aluminum ladders. Available in total lengths from 16 to 40 feet, extension ladders are normally purchased for their ''working'' lengths—that is, the distance from the ladder's top support to the ground when the ladder is set against a building at a 75-degree angle. The working length is a few feet less than the total length.

Selecting a good ladder

All ladders are subject to use-rated standards set by the government and industry associations. Type III are household-grade ladders rated at 200 pounds. Type II are commercial-grade and rated at 225 pounds. Type I are industrial, with a 250-pound rating. Each type has passed tests at four times the specified loads. The grade will be specified on the side rails. For long-lasting reliability, select at least a Type II.

The difference between wood and aluminum ladders is cost and weight. Aluminum ladders cost more, but are a lot easier to maneuver.

The length you should choose depends upon the use you intend to put the ladder to. An extension ladder whose working length won't reach the top portions of your home will have limited use for you. For access to lower levels, as well as for inside work, a 6- to 8-foot stepladder is very useful. No matter what length you're considering, remember that it's better to buy a longer ladder than risk an accident caused by overreaching.

When you need scaffolding

Scaffolds are temporary or movable platforms that allow you to work on large high areas both safely and comfortably, with both hands free. They can be built from solid 2-inch lumber, fabricated with jacks and ladders, or rented as modular, manufactured units. If you are less than expert about ladders and construction techniques, consider renting a scaffold when you need one.

PUTTING UP A LADDER

Setting up an extension ladder at first seems like a juggling act, but before long you'll get the feel of it. The first time, have a helper on hand to protect against slips and tipping, and to steady the ladder as you go up and down.

1 To set up a ladder, place its feet against the foundation or other base. Grasp a rung at the upper end with both hands, then raise the ladder and walk forward under it, moving from rung to rung.

2 Raise an extension ladder by bracing the bottom with your foot, lifting the ladder out from the house, and pulling the rope until the ladder is high enough. Be sure the locks holding the sections together catch securely.

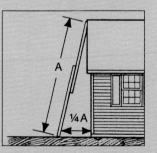

3 With the ladder extended and in place, check that its base is on level ground and about one-fourth of its working length is out from the building. The top rails should rest evenly against their support. The ladder should not rock.

MOVING AROUND ON A ROOF

Roofs weren't designed to be walked upon, and unless you exercise care, you'll damage roofing materials and possibly yourself.

Be sure to wear sneakers and walk only on a dry roof. Stay off a roof during windy days, too, and don't touch power lines.

Use a straight ladder or half an extension. Hook a stabilizer bar over the ridge, or tie ropes to the top rung and fasten them to a tree on the other side.

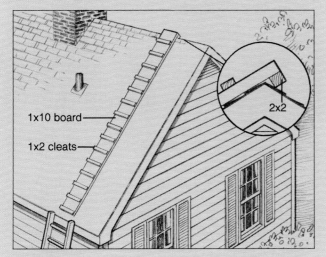

1x10 board

1x2 cleats

2x2

To fabricate a ladder that will evenly distribute your weight, nail 1x2 cleats to one side of a 1x10 board, and a 2x2 to the other. Lay it on the roof as shown.

LADDER SAFETY BASICS

Using a ladder safely calls for common sense, not rigid rules. Here are some basic guidelines to follow.
- Keep ladders in working order by oiling moving parts and tightening nuts and bolts. Don't make "temporary" repairs, and never use a bent or straightened metal ladder—it will be weak.
- Set the ladder close enough to the place you're working on to avoid overreaching.
- Keep your weight centered between the side rails, and lean toward the rungs for stability.
- Always face the ladder when ascending or descending; don't proceed as if you were on a conventional stairway.
- For safety, a ladder's feet must always stand on a firm, level surface. Don't level the feet with small shims, boards, or stones that could shift as you climb.
- Steps and rungs should be free of oil, grease, paint, and other slippery substances.
- Never set up a ladder in front of a door or other opening unless you've blocked it off from traffic.
- For safety, overlap extension ladder sections by the following lengths: 3 feet for 36 feet of extended length; 4 feet for up to 48 feet; and 5 feet for a length up to 60 feet.
- Never stand on the top three rungs of an extension ladder.
- Don't stand or climb on the top, pail rest, or rear rungs of a stepladder.
- Never adjust the height of an extension from the ladder. Climb down and raise or lower the ladder.
- Double-check both locks on extension ladder rungs before climbing.
- Never use a metal ladder or wet wooden one where there is danger of contact with a live electric wire.
- Avoid using tall ladders on windy days.
- For stability, use stepladders fully open, with their spreaders straight.
- Don't overload any type of ladder. Ladders are intended to be used by one person at a time.
- Never paint a wooden ladder; the paint could hide future defects.
- Use ladders only as they're meant to be used. Horizontal use can weaken them.
- Store ladders in dry ventilated places, such as on the rafters in a garage. Keep them out of reach of burglars who might use a ladder for access to upper-level windows.
- If you suspect a ladder's structural integrity, don't use it.

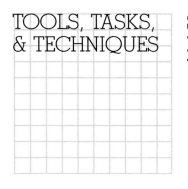

STAYING
IN TUNE
WITH NATURE

Before settlements re-placed the wilderness on this continent, nature reg-ulated the growing cycle of trees, shrubs, and other vege-tation. Outside your home, the process continues, although on a smaller scale. Trees grow and die; wild creatures make do with what they have—which may be your garden—and ter-mites, lacking the dead wood of a forest, turn to your house instead. To enjoy nature's presence outside your home, you must exercise some con-trol over it. To learn about con-trolling wildlife, see the facing page; to learn about managing your own private "forest," read on.

Trees require regular, even annual attention if they are to contribute fully to your land-scaping. Be sure to have dead or dying trees removed promptly, to avoid the danger of a wind-felled tree doing seri-ous damage to your home or a passerby. If you're in doubt about the health of any of your trees, consult a local nursery-man or government forester. Leave tree removal to experts.

Pruning in very early spring or late fall will prevent shrubs and trees from becoming over-grown. In many cases, pruning helps develop their symmetry and prevents possible threats to power lines, roofing, and siding. Pruning also is good for the trees, usually encouraging more energetic growth.

If you have dead branches or limbs that seem to pose a hazard, you should be able to deal with them yourself, unless they're very high. The illustra-tions *at right* show how to remove a dead or dangerous limb and help heal the result-ing wound to the tree or shrub.

PRUNING TREE LIMBS

1 Don't try to saw off an entire limb with one cut. Make your first cut about a foot or so from the trunk. Cut one-quarter of the way through from the underside, and stop when the saw begins to bind. A long and heavy limb may need to be secured with a rope before cutting.

2 Go to the top side of the limb and start your second cut about 4 inches out from the first. Begin to slowly saw all the way through. With a larger limb, you may want to step back before it gives way in order to avoid any rebound. As the limb falls, the bark will strip away to your first cut.

3 Next, remove the re-maining stub by sawing as flush with the trunk as possible while supporting the stub with your free hand. Watch that the falling stub doesn't strip bark from the trunk and further wound the tree. Never leave a stub—it will decay and fun-nel insects or disease into the tree's heart.

4 Trim loose bark from the edge of the wound with a sharp knife, then paint the area with tree wound dress-ing to disinfect the area and keep moisture out. Until the wound heals naturally, apply the dressing every spring and fall. Healing will be marked by a gradual closing of the bark sur-rounding the wound.

WATCH OUT FOR TERMITES

Termites are defined as social insects, but you certainly don't want them as guests in your house; they feast on wood components. Termites once were pretty much limited to mild and temperate zones, but they've spread northward in recent years, so you need to be on the lookout for them almost everywhere.

In spring and fall, reproductive members of termite colonies sprout wings, fly around in search of mates, and then discard the wings before nesting. If you spot a pile of wings near your home, you may well have a colony nearby.

Termites look similar to ants, but have thick waistlines and—in their reproductive phase—two pairs of equal-length wings. Don't confuse them with flying ants, which don't eat wood. The drawings below illustrate the differences between termites and flying ants.

Older homes often have traces of past termite damage, but these don't necessarily indicate that termites are still present. Newly built homes often feature termite shields, which are installed during construction. These shields are simply wide sheets of metal, placed between the foundation and the sill plate to keep termites away from aboveground wood. Shields are not guarantees against infestation, so watch out for telltale signs even if your home is constructed with a shield.

Types of termites

Subterranean termites, the most voracious type, live in the ground. The workers make daily trips from their belowground nests to climb toward the nearest supply of cellulose. To avoid exposure to the elements and to secure a route, they often build mud tunnels from the ground up the foundation to the wood supply. Keep an eye open for their sheltered tubes.

Nonsubterranean termites, as well as powder-post beetles and carpenter ants, live in the wood itself in a limited area such as a wood column or doorframe. These insects are less destructive than subterranean termites. Often you can spot their entrance holes, which are marked by piles of sawdust. A large nest of these insects will be noisy enough to hear when they're chewing, though you may have to put your ear to the wood to hear them.

You can check for suspected termite damage in beams, joists, and other framing members by poking an awl or other sharply pointed tool into the wood. If you discover large, hollow spaces, call a licensed exterminator. Termites can destroy a house in time if not properly eliminated.

General procedures

All extermination procedures call for chemical treatment on a regular basis. The chemicals used are extremely toxic if mishandled or misapplied, so leave termite control to a reputable professional. You should, however, be familiar with the procedure.

Eliminating subterranean termites involves surrounding a foundation with an underground moat of insecticide. Special equipment is used to inject it into the ground, where the chemical isolates the termites from their food. Termite workers who are in the house cannot get back to their colony and soon die.

Nonsubterranean termites, powder-post beetles, and carpenter ants are somewhat easier to dispense with. Holes are bored into the infested area and a chemical in either powder or liquid form is sprayed in.

Treatment for all types of wood-boring insects normally includes periodic inspections and follow-up spraying as necessary. Most reputable exterminators guarantee their work for several years and make annual inspections.

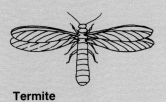

Termite

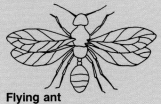

Flying ant

HOW TO CONTROL OTHER PESTS

Winged and furry creatures can be charming to watch, but they also can be nuisances if they attack your home's exterior or get inside. To guard against attic occupancy by squirrels, bats, or birds, screen all potential entrances with hardware cloth or other substantial material. Gable vents, roof-top ventilators, and soffit vents should be checked each year to be sure they're adequately screened.

Cut back tree branches near your home so they can't serve as launching pads for squirrels or raccoons who'd like to take up residence in your chimney. To keep these creatures, as well as birds, out of your chimney, you should have a screened cap over it, too. Be sure to check the cap occasionally to be sure it's not blocked.

One type of bird poses another problem: Woodpeckers can drum holes into wood siding, usually in search of insects that live in the wood. You can try to keep the insects, and thus the woodpeckers, away by applying insecticide or preservative to the wood. If that doesn't work, scare the birds away with bird-of-prey decoys or foil strips.

COPING WITH WEATHER'S WORST

No matter where you choose to live, your home and property may at one time or another be assaulted by the elements. Tornadoes, mud slides, brush-fires, hurricanes, thunder-storms, and blizzards are familiar enemies in various parts of the country. There's nothing you can do to prevent most of these natural disasters, of course, but there are things you can do to lessen their impact.

Windstorms

Tornadoes, those twisting col-umns of wind that often drop down from a severe storm front in spring and summer, can be predicted. Because they travel in erratic paths, however, you can never be quite sure that a tornado will reach you. If you live in an area where tornadoes are common, you should have a designated place inside your home to serve as a storm shelter.

A basement corner is the best choice, although there's continuing debate over which compass corner you should choose. Whatever the corner, be sure it's protected by beams and joists above. Keep a battery-powered radio, a supply of drinking water, a dependable flashlight, extra batteries, a shovel, ax or saw, ropes, and nonperishable dried or canned food in that corner.

Hurricanes are similar in ef-fect to tornadoes, but because they're primarily coastal storms, they are accompanied by high tides and often floods. Boarding up windows with sheets of plywood, tying every-thing down or putting it inside, then going inland by car is the normal procedure for dealing with approaching hurricanes.

Other calamities

Floods. Unless they come without warning, as flash floods in desert regions are apt to, floods can be less damaging to your home than you'd think. If you're expecting flooding, there are several pro-tective measures you can take. Erect plywood barriers; use heavy plastic sheets to trap water and cover damageable items; place sandbags strategi-cally to divert water away from your home. Keep food, water, lights, tools, and flotation de-vices on hand for emergency use. If you live in a flood-prone area, you might consider in-stalling check valves in sewer drains to prevent backups.

Electrical storms are so familiar that we don't always think of them in the same cate-gory as other natural disasters. But they can be severe, caus-ing damage to homes and other property, killing livestock and occasionally people.

Much of the damage caused by lightning results from electri-cal surges, which enter the house from overhead power lines and cables. Surging can destroy motors in appliances, ruin television sets and radios, and burn out electrical wires. Surge protectors are installed on fuse boxes or circuit break-ers where power enters the house. These must be installed on hot wires, so the work is best left to an electrician. In areas where electrical storms occur frequently or severely, you should have the protection of a professionally installed grounding system, like that illustrated *opposite.* If electrical storms are not a serious prob-lem where you live, you can install antenna ground wires and lightning arresters yourself. Both are available at electrical supply stores.

WARDING OFF ICE DAMS AND SNOW SLIDES

If you live in a cold or snowy area, accumulations of ice and snow on the roof can cause problems. On gently sloping roofs, snow often melts from the bottom, letting water run freely un-der a blanket of snow until it reaches the eaves. There, contact with colder air out-side the blanket causes the water to freeze and build up in successive layers. The result is an ice dam that can back water up under the shingles, cause an inside leak, and damage the sheathing. If your roof is prone to ice dams, consid-er installing low-voltage heating cables along the eaves, as some homeown-ers do. These melt some of the ice, allowing the water to flow into the gutters and drain away.

Steeply pitched roofs sel-dom have ice dam prob-lems, because the water runs off fast. They do, how-ever, present the possibility of slides if the snow is heavy enough. Huge sheets of snow can break loose and cascade down, often tearing off pieces of roofing or gutters and damaging foundation plantings. Snow guards, illustrated *below,* disrupt sliding snow and break it into harmless small-er chunks as it slides.

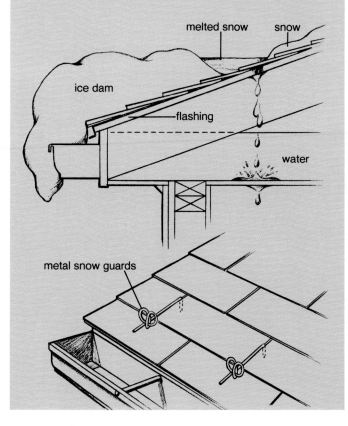

melted snow

snow

ice dam

flashing

water

metal snow guards

PROTECTING AGAINST LIGHTNING

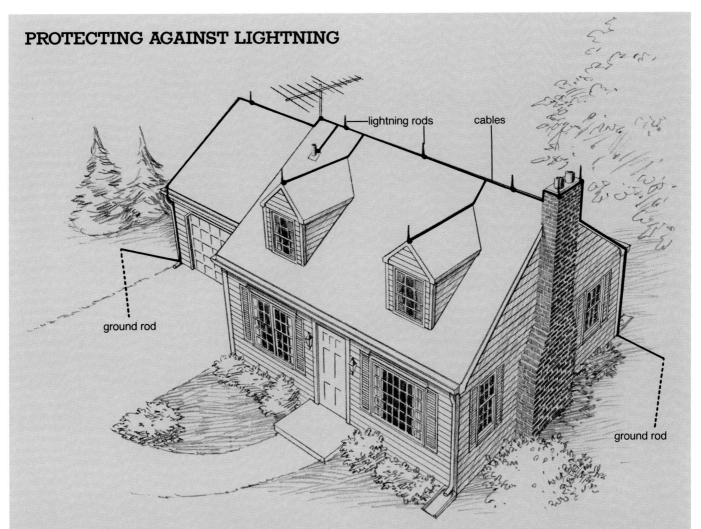

lightning rods

cables

ground rod

ground rod

Lightning, like all electrical energy, seeks the shortest path into the ground. The purpose of a lightning protection system is to intercept lightning that otherwise might travel through your house. When lightning strikes, it is diverted to rods placed on the chimney, ridges, antennas (if any), gutters, and flashings. From the rods, the lightning's electrical current is carried by heavy-gauge copper or aluminum cable to a pair of ground rods driven into the earth at opposite ends of the building.

Trees and other prominent features that stand taller than your home and are located close to it are similarly treated, not to protect them, but to prevent lightning from jumping to the house in case they are struck.

Any lightning protection system you have installed should meet the standards of the National Fire Protection Association and Underwriters Laboratories. Make sure this will be the case before you have the system installed. Also arrange to have an expert check the system every few years.

If you believe your home or outbuildings may be particularly susceptible to lightning strikes because of their size, location, or degree of isolation, the cost of a protection system will be well worthwhile just for your peace of mind. In addition, you may receive a discount on your homeowners' insurance.

WHERE TO GO FOR MORE INFORMATION

Better Homes and Gardens® Books

Would you like to learn more about planning and maximizing the outdoor spaces at your house? These Better Homes and Gardens® books can help.

Better Homes and Gardens®
COMPLETE GUIDE TO HOME REPAIR,
MAINTENANCE, & IMPROVEMENT
Inside your home, outside your home, your home's systems, basics you should know. Anatomy and step-by-step drawings illustrate components, tools, techniques, and finishes.
515 how-to techniques; 75 charts; 2,734 illustrations; 552 pages.

Better Homes and Gardens®
COMPLETE GUIDE TO GARDENING
A comprehensive guide for beginners and experienced gardeners. Houseplants, lawns and landscaping, trees and shrubs, greenhouses, insects and diseases. 461 color photos, 434 how-to illustrations, 37 charts, 552 pages.

Better Homes and Gardens®
STEP-BY-STEP BUILDING SERIES
A series of do-it-yourself building books that provides step-by-step illustrations and how-to information for starting and finishing many common construction projects and repair jobs around your house. More than 90 projects and 1,200 illustrations in this series of six 96-page books:
STEP-BY-STEP BASIC CARPENTRY
STEP-BY-STEP BASIC WIRING
STEP-BY-STEP BASIC PLUMBING
STEP-BY-STEP MASONRY & CONCRETE
STEP-BY-STEP CABINETS & SHELVES
STEP-BY-STEP HOUSEHOLD REPAIRS

Other Sources of Information

Many professional associations will provide lists of their members to interested consumers; several special-interest associations and manufacturers publish catalogs, style books, and product brochures that are available upon request. Addresses, and charges, if any, were current at the time this book was published but may have changed.

American Hardboard
 Association (AHA)
887-B Wilmette Road
Palatine, IL 60067

American Plywood
 Association
7011 S. 19th Street
P.O. Box 11700
Tacoma, WA 98411

Asphalt Roofing
 Manufacturers
 Association
6288 Montrose Road
Rockville, MD 20852

"A Homeowners Guide to the
 Selection of Quality Roofing
 Materials"
Send 50 cents per copy to
Asphalt Roofing
 Manufacturers
 Association
P.O. Box 3248
New York, NY 10163

Information on vinyl siding:
Bird Incorporated
Withrow Lane
Bardstown, KY 40004

California Redwood
 Association
591 Redwood Highway,
 Suite 3100
Mill Valley, CA 94941

Cellulose Manufacturers
 Association (CMA)
5908 Columbia Pike
Baileys Crossroads, VA
 22041

Gypsum Association
1603 Orrington Avenue
Evanston, IL 60201

Red Cedar Shingle &
 Handsplit Shake Bureau
515-116th Avenue N.E.
Suite 275
Bellevue, WA 98004

The Stanley Works (tools)
Dept. BHG
P.O. Box 1800
New Britain, CT 06050

Western Wood Products
 Association
1500 Yeon Building
Portland, OR 97204

ACKNOWLEDGMENTS

Architects and Designers

The following is a page-by-page listing of the interior designers, architects, and project designers whose work appears in this book.

Pages 6-7
  Marc Tarasuck and
  Associates AIA
Pages 8-9
  James Hriko
Pages 12-13
  Michael Ritter, Exterior
  Design Studio
Pages 14-15
  Loren Gardner Landscape,
  Jan Hougen, Kidder
  Nursery, left;
  Topher Delaney, right
Pages 18-19
  Barbara Fealy
Pages 20-21
  Thomas H. Olson
Page 40
  Thomas E. Eldridge, left
Pages 42-43
  Henry and Eunice Thomas,
  left; Claude Shuttey, right

Pages 44-45
  Architectural Period Homes
  Inc., left; Elwood and
  Elsie Lorey, right
Pages 46-47
  Jefferson Riley, Moore
  Grover Harper P.C., top
  right; Batey & Mack
Pages 52-53
  Rasmussen and Hobbs
Pages 54-55
  Kaye Halverson, Touch of
  Class Interiors
Pages 60-61
  Loren Gardener Landscape,
  Jan Hougen, Kidder Nursery
Pages 66-67
  Don Christensen
Pages 70-71
  John Milnes Baker, left;
  Jacqueline Williams, right
Pages 72-73
  Chuck Dunseth
Pages 76-77
  Fisher Friedman
  Associates AIA
Pages 98-99
  Richard Wills AIA
Pages 102-105
  Asphalt Roofing Manufac-
  turers Association
Pages 106-109
  Masonite Corporation
Pages 110-111
  Michael R. Van
  Valkenburgh ASLA

Pages 112-113
  Julia Lundy, upper left;
  Karlis Grants, lower left;
  M. Dean Jones, right
Pages 114-115
  Mary Ellen Suter
Pages 116-117
  Jill Van Tosh
Pages 120-121
  Ailine Millar ASID
Pages 124-125
  Timberline Design,
  Woodbutcher
Pages 126-127
  John Berhst, Jr.
Pages 130-131
  George C. Fuller; Richard
  Kaleh and Associates
Pages 132-133
  John Nicol
Pages 134-135
  Timberline Design,
  Woodbutcher
Pages 136-137
  Michael Ritter, Exterior
  Design Studio
Pages 138-139
  James Sinatra ASLA
Pages 140-145
  Sal Vasques

Manufacturers and Associations

We extend our thanks to the following manufacturers and associations who contributed to this book.

Asphalt Roofing Manufacturers
  Association
American Wood Council
California Redwood
  Association
Bird Incorporated
Western Wood Products
  Association

Photographers and Illustrators

We extend our thanks to the following photographers and illustrators whose creative talents and technical skills contributed to this book.

Ernest Braun
George Ceolla
Ross Chapple
George de Gennaro
Karlis Grants
William N. Hopkins
Bill Hopkins, Jr.
Scott Little
Fred Lyon
Maris/Semel
E. Alan McGee
Stephen Mead
Frank Lotz Miller
Joe Standart
Ozzie Sweet
John Vaughan

INDEX

Page numbers in *italics* refer to photographs or illustrated text.

INDEX
(continued)